THE COMPLETE GUIDE TO THE
50 STATES

NANCY DICKMANN

An Imprint of Sterling Publishing Co., Inc.
1166 Avenue of the Americas
New York, NY 10036

Text © 2016 by QEB Publishing, Inc.
Illustrations © 2016 by QEB Publishing, Inc.

ISBN: 978-1-4351-6358-4

Manufactured in Guangdong, China
Lot #:
4   6   8   10 9   7   5   3
03/18

www.sterlingpublishing.com

THE COMPLETE GUIDE TO THE
50 STATES

NANCY DICKMANN

Sandy Creek
NEW YORK

CONTENTS

FROM SEA TO SHINING SEA

Stretching from the Atlantic Ocean to the Pacific, the United States of America is the fourth-largest country in the world, home to more than 300 million people. It is a land of contrasts, made up of 50 different states. Each state has its own unique character, but together they work to form a powerful, united nation.

Yosemite National Park, California, is one of 58 protected National Parks in the United States.

Coast to Coast

The landscape of the United States ranges from majestic snow-capped mountains in the west, through vast **prairies** in the central part, to the forested, swampy southeast. You can find virtually every type of landform somewhere in the United States: hills, deserts, coasts, lakes, **glaciers**, and more. Mighty rivers crisscross the land, while roads and railroad tracks link the cities.

Each of the 50 states has its own flag, customs, and traditions.

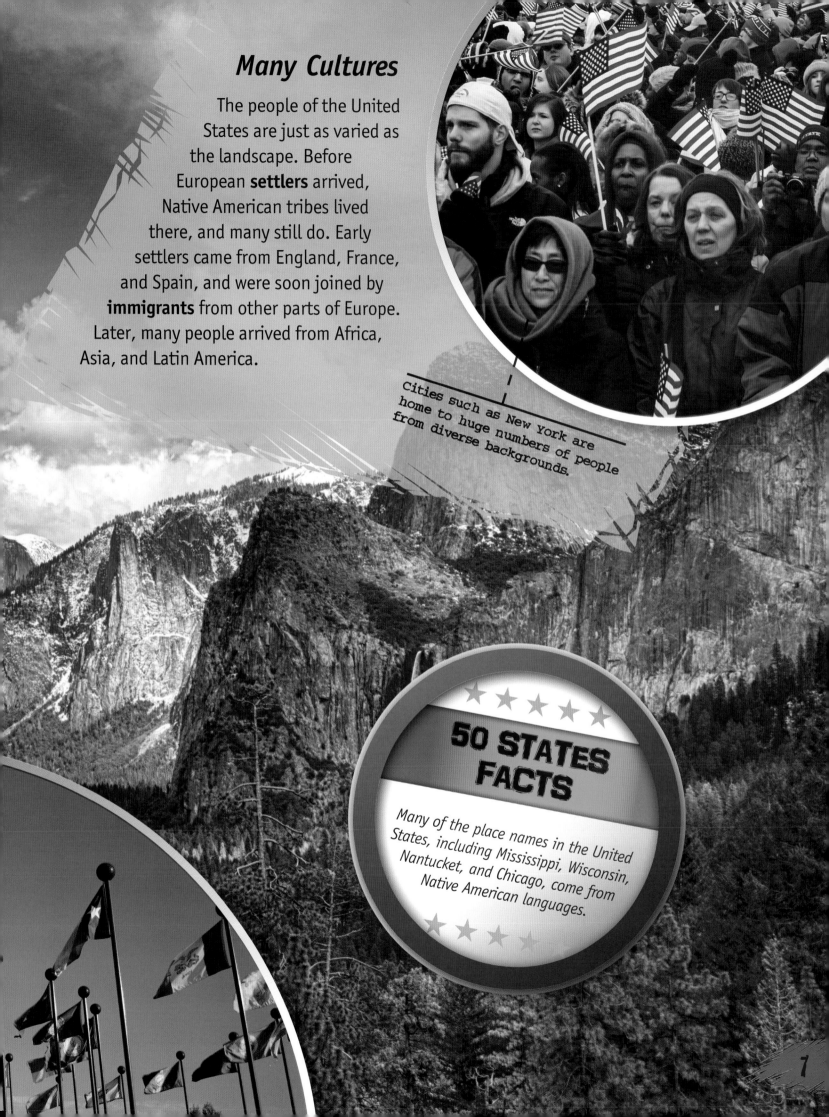

Many Cultures

The people of the United States are just as varied as the landscape. Before European **settlers** arrived, Native American tribes lived there, and many still do. Early settlers came from England, France, and Spain, and were soon joined by **immigrants** from other parts of Europe. Later, many people arrived from Africa, Asia, and Latin America.

Cities such as New York are home to huge numbers of people from diverse backgrounds.

50 STATES FACTS

Many of the place names in the United States, including Mississippi, Wisconsin, Nantucket, and Chicago, come from Native American languages.

THE 13 COLONIES

When the English first arrived on the east coast in the 17th century, they organized their new settlements into 13 separate **colonies**. The English government controlled these colonies, and the rich land provided important natural resources such as timber, furs, and crops that could be sent back to England.

Captain John Smith helped to found Jamestown, the first permanent English settlement.

Changing Times

Over the years, the populations in the colonies grew. Eventually, many of the people who had been born there saw themselves as American rather than English. They loved the freedom and opportunities available in North America. However, the colonists had to pay **taxes** to England, and they had no voice in the government. Many of them began to think that this was unfair. They thought that the colonies should be free to govern themselves.

This famous painting of musicians marching across a battlefield shows the pride of the colonists in their new nation.

Breaking Free

Tensions rose, and fighting began. In 1776, a group of men representing each of the 13 colonies signed the Declaration of Independence. This document declared that the colonies were now independent of England. There were years of fierce fighting, but eventually the colonists were able to drive the British soldiers out of the country. After the war ended, the 13 colonies became the first states.

The colonists wrote a **constitution** that set out how the new country's government would work.

50 STATES FACTS

Each colony had to **ratify**, or approve, the constitution before it could go into effect. Delaware was first to ratify it, on December 7, 1787, becoming the first state.

Early settlers had to work hard to clear land for farming.

9

MOVING WEST

As the population of the new country grew, settlers moved farther and farther west, into land that was once wilderness. Life there could be hard, and settlers often came into conflict with the Native Americans who lived there. But they worked hard to set up farms and towns, and some of these new territories soon became states.

New States

Vermont became the 14th state in 1791, and it was followed by Kentucky and Tennessee. Like the original 13, each of these new states had organized its population to write a state constitution and create a state government with the power to run elections, regulate trade, and take part in federal decisions. Once **Congress** had accepted the constitution, the new territory was accepted as a state.

When Vermont became a state, there were just 85,425 people living there.

FREEDOM VERMONT AND UNITY

The Country Grows

In 1803, President Thomas Jefferson (1743–1826) bought a huge area of land, west of the Mississippi River, from France. This region was called the Louisiana **Territory**, and its purchase doubled the size of the country. American settlers soon moved in, living side by side with the British and French **trappers** and traders who were already there. Many new states, including Iowa, Kansas, and Arkansas, were eventually formed from this land.

Meriwether Lewis (shown here) and William Clark were sent by President Jefferson to lead an expedition to explore the **Louisiana Purchase.**

50 STATES FACTS

Starting in the 17th century, traders brought enslaved men, women, and children from Africa to work on farms in colonies. In some states, **slavery** lasted until the end of the **Civil War** (1865).

The mighty Mississippi River starts in Minnesota and runs south to Louisiana. It forms the eastern boundary of the Louisiana Territory.

BEYOND THE MISSISSIPPI

In the 19th century, the population of the United States swelled as immigrants poured in from Germany, Ireland, and other countries. People were drawn by the opportunity to own their own land and live in freedom. These settlers pushed west, eventually reaching the Pacific Coast. Between 1812 and 1896, 28 new states were formed.

The rush of new immigrants led to the growth of cities such as New York, shown here in 1900.

The Oregon Trail

Many settlers followed the **Oregon Trail**, a 2,200-mile route that connected the eastern states to the new territory of Oregon. Whole families made the trip, traveling on foot, on horseback, or in large covered wagons. The difficult journey involved crossing the Rocky Mountains, and many settlers did not make it. But those that did settled in western regions that eventually became states.

When the Transcontinental Railroad was completed in 1869, the journey west became much easier.

Some of the landscapes in the west, such as Monument Valley in Utah, were very different from the settlers' original homes.

Whenever new states joined the USA, the flag had to be updated. A version with 48 stars was used from 1912 to 1959.

Fifty at Last

In 1912, New Mexico and Arizona became the 47th and 48th states. Now all the land between Canada and Mexico was fully divided into different states. Some people thought there would be no more new states. But in 1959, two more were added. Alaska was bought from Russia back in 1867, and Hawaii had been taken over in the 1890s. Both were territories before they became states.

50 STATES FACTS

The land in the western United States was home to many Native Americans, as well as Mexicans and settlers from other countries. Many of them were forced from their lands by the new settlers.

13

TIMELINE OF STATEHOOD

After winning its independence, it took more than 170 years for the United States to grow from one state to 50. This map shows when the new states were added.

This key shows when the states on the map were formed. Each state is colored according to the time period in which it was formed.

- 1787-1790
- 1791-1803
- 1812-1821
- 1836-1859
- 1861-1890
- 1896-1959

WASHINGTON
1889

MONTANA
1889

NORTH DAKOTA
1889

OREGON
1859

IDAHO
1890

SOUTH DAKOTA
1889

WYOMING
1890

NEBRASKA
1867

NEVADA
1864

UTAH
1896

COLORADO
1876

CALIFORNIA
1850

ARIZONA
1912

NEW MEXICO
1912

TEXAS
1845

ALASKA
1959

HAWAII
1959

From Territory to State

Many states were territories before they became states. When new areas were bought or ceded to the United States, they were usually organized into a territory. Once enough settlers had moved there, a referendum would determine whether the residents wanted statehood. The territory had to adopt a constitution before applying for statehood. Many states were carved out of areas such as the **Northwest Territory**, the Louisiana Territory, and the Oregon Territory.

MINNESOTA
1858

MICHIGAN
1837

WISCONSIN
1848

NEW HAMPSHIRE
1788

MAINE
1820

VERMONT
1791

MASSACHUSETTS
1788

IOWA
1846

NEW YORK
1788

RHODE ISLAND
1790

CONNECTICUT
1788

PENNSYLVANIA
1787

ILLINOIS
1818

INDIANA
1816

OHIO
1803

NEW JERSEY
1787

DELAWARE
1787

WEST VIRGINIA
1863

VIRGINIA
1788

MARYLAND
1788

ANSAS
1861

MISSOURI
1821

KENTUCKY
1792

KLAHOMA
1907

ARKANSAS
1836

TENNESSEE
1796

NORTH CAROLINA
1789

SOUTH CAROLINA
1788

GEORGIA
1788

ALABAMA
1819

MISSISSIPPI
1817

LOUISIANA
1812

FLORIDA
1845

50 STATES FACTS

It has been more than 50 years since the last new state was added. The second-longest gap between states joining was 47 years, from Arizona in 1912 to Alaska in 1959.

REGIONS AND TERRITORIES

The states can be divided roughly into regions. In this book, they have been put into groups that often share a similar landscape, culture, or economy. These divisions are not official, and they do not affect how the country is run. In government, each state stands alone.

The 48 contiguous states are split into four time zones.

Parts of the states that include the Appalachian Mountains make up an unofficial region called Appalachia.

Different Divisions

There are many different ways of dividing up the country. The Census Bureau, which is in charge of counting and analyzing the country's population, divides the country into four regions—Northeast, Midwest, South, and West—that are split into nine subdivisions. Other regions, such as Appalachia, include only parts of states.

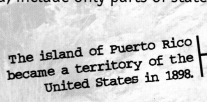
The island of Puerto Rico became a territory of the United States in 1898.

Territories

The United States also includes land that is not organized into states. Territories are areas that are overseen by the **federal government**, but which do not have **representatives** who can vote in Congress. U.S. territories include the islands of Puerto Rico, Guam, the U.S. Virgin Islands, and American Samoa. Residents of some territories are U.S. citizens, while some others are classed as U.S. nationals. People in the territories cannot vote in presidential elections.

The territory of Wake Island, in the Pacific Ocean, is used as a base by the U.S. Air Force.

50 STATES FACTS

The list of U.S. territories includes several small islands in the Caribbean Sea and Pacific Ocean with no permanent populations. These include Baker Island, Howland Island, and Jarvis Island.

NEW ENGLAND

The region of New England contains some of the first European settlements in North America. The **Pilgrims** from England founded the Plymouth Colony in 1620, and the city of Boston was founded 10 years later. The colonies of New England played an important role in the fight for independence from the British.

The New England region is famous for its beautiful fall colors.

Landscape

Compared to other regions, New England is small, and its states include Maine, New Hampshire, Vermont, Massachusetts, Connecticut, and Rhode Island. It is a beautiful area, with mountains, rivers, forests, and a jagged Atlantic coastline. Much of the landscape was shaped during the last **ice age**, when glaciers scraped across the land. Most parts of the region have cold winters with heavy snowfall, and a fairly short summer.

Small wooden churches, often painted white, are a common sight in the New England countryside.

People and Industry

New England is very densely populated, with nearly 15 million people packed into a fairly small area. Many of its residents share a similar European ancestry, and over the centuries this has shaped their distinct accent, customs, and food. In the past, the long coastline meant that whaling and fishing were important industries. In the 19th century, many factories were built, especially textile mills. Now the region is known for high-tech research and education.

New England's rocky coast is popular with tourists, but its rich waters are also an important source of income.

50 STATES FACTS

New England's borders with the Canadian province of Quebec have given New England's culture a strong French influence. In some parts, many people still speak French as their first language.

MAINE

At the far northeastern tip of the country is the state of Maine. It is famous for its rugged coastline, beautiful beaches, and dense forests, but it also has a rich and varied history. As the easternmost point of the United States, it is where the nation's day begins. It was originally part of Massachusetts, but it **seceded** to become a separate state in 1820.

Acadia National Park protects more than 47,000 acres of wilderness.

Lobster fishing is an important industry in Maine, producing more than 100 million pounds per year.

Forests and Coasts

Approximately 83 percent of the land in Maine is covered in forest, which gives it the nickname "The Pine Tree State." These parts of the state are very sparsely populated. Maine has almost 230 miles of coast, featuring lighthouses, beaches, and many small islands. Acadia National Park covers parts of several islands just off the coast. It is home to many different plants, as well as moose, beaver, deer, and black bears.

Maine's moose population is estimated at around 70,000.

MAINE FACT FILE

Admitted to Union: 1820 (the 23rd state)
Capital: Augusta
Rank in size: 39th
Rank in population: 41st
Nickname: Pine Tree State

People of Maine

Most residents of Maine are of European ancestry, and more than half the population is of French, English, or Irish descent. Maine has the highest percentage of native French speakers among U.S. states. It has been home to many writers, poets, and artists, and some of their work shows the struggle of people against the rugged natural features of the land.

NEW HAMPSHIRE

New Hampshire's history began in 1623, when a group of English settlers founded a fishing colony near the mouth of the Piscataqua River. It was named after the county of Hampshire in England. New Hampshire was the first of the 13 colonies to adopt its own constitution, and the first to declare independence from England. After independence, it became the first state to establish a public library.

The granite rocks of the White Mountains give the state its nickname.

New Hampshire's official motto is a quote from John Stark, a general in the **Revolutionary War.**

Welcome   Bienvenue
New Hampshire
"Live Free or Die"

NEW HAMPSHIRE FACT FILE

Admitted to Union: 1788 (the 9th state)
Capital: Concord
Rank in size: 46th
Rank in population: 42nd
Nickname: Granite State

Inhabitants

Like Maine, most of New Hampshire's population is of French, English, or Irish descent. Relatively few people live in the northern part of the state. The most densely populated areas are in the south, and many residents commute to Boston or other cities in Massachusetts. In the past, New Hampshire's economy depended on granite quarries, lumber, and paper. Now, tourists come to the state for skiing, snowboarding, and hiking.

The purple finch is the state bird of New Hampshire. Only the males are brightly colored.

Mountains and Streams

New Hampshire is small, but several important rivers have their sources in its granite hills. Forests cover much of the land, and the White Mountains rise in the north-central part of the state. Mount Washington, the highest peak, is also the tallest mountain in New England. New Hampshire has borders with Quebec, Maine, Vermont, and Massachusetts, and it has the shortest coastline of any state, at just 18 miles.

VERMONT

Vermont was not one of the original 13 colonies. The land was settled by the French and then surrendered to England in 1763. Colonists from neighboring New York and New Hampshire both tried to control the area. In 1777, a group of men signed the Constitution of Vermont. It declared Vermont to be an independent state. This Vermont **Republic** lasted until 1791, when it joined the newly formed United States as the 14th state.

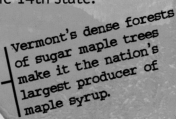

Vermont's dense forests of sugar maple trees make it the nation's largest producer of maple syrup.

A Rugged Wilderness

Vermont is the only state in New England not to border the Atlantic Ocean, but it does have a long lake coastline on the west, where Lake Champlain separates it from New York. Most of the state's land is rocky and mountainous, and the tree-covered Green Mountains make up a large part of the state. As a result, little of the land is suitable for farming, although dairy cattle make up a very important part of the state's economy.

Progressive Ideas

Vermont has a long history of supporting human rights and individual liberty. It was the first state to ban slavery, and one of the first to give women the right to vote. More recently, it became the first state to give full marriage rights to same-sex couples. The state is very rural, and much of the population lives in small towns and villages. The biggest city, Burlington, has fewer than 50,000 residents.

In 2015, Burlington became the first major U.S. city to run entirely on renewable energy.

The Green Mountains are home to several winter sports resorts.

VERMONT FACT FILE

Admitted to Union: 1791 (the 14th state)
Capital: Montpelier
Rank in size: 45th
Rank in population: 49th
Nickname: Green Mountain State

MASSACHUSETTS

Massachusetts has played an important role in the country's history. The first permanent English settlement, Plymouth, was founded here in 1620. Boston became one of the most important cities in the colonies, and many key events in the struggle for independence, such as the Boston Tea Party and the Battles of Lexington and Concord, took place in Massachusetts. Even after the Revolutionary War, Massachusetts remained influential.

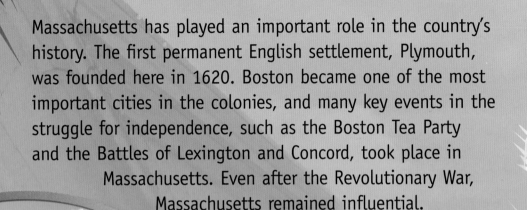

Harvard University, in Cambridge, was the first college in North America.

Shaped by the Sea

Sandwiched between Vermont and New Hampshire to the north, and Connecticut and Rhode Island to the south, Massachusetts has a long coastline. The **peninsula** of Cape Cod curls out into the ocean, and islands such as Nantucket and Martha's Vineyard make up part of the state. This geography made Massachusetts a center for the whaling industry. Away from the coast, hills and valleys lead westward to the Berkshire Mountains.

MASSACHUSETTS FACT FILE

Admitted to Union: 1788 (the 6th state)
Capital: Boston
Rank in size: 44th
Rank in population: 14th
Nickname: Bay State

Boston has many historic buildings dating from colonial times, such as Faneuil Hall.

Population

Massachusetts is the third-most densely populated state, and it has a diverse population. There are many people of Irish descent, and the St. Patrick's Day parade is an annual tradition. Boston is by far the largest city, with nearly five million people living in the metro area. Massachusetts' many universities and research labs give it a reputation as a center for high-tech industry.

There are many cranberry bogs in Massachusetts, making it the nation's second-largest producer of these tart red berries.

CONNECTICUT

Colonists from Massachusetts moved into the region that is now Connecticut in the 1630s. Soon after, it was the site of the Pequot War (1636–1637), one of the first major conflicts between the settlers and Native American tribes. In 1639, residents of the colony wrote the Fundamental Orders, considered to be the first constitution in the colonies, giving Connecticut its nickname of the "Constitution State."

The tree known as the "Charter Oak" stood in Connecticut until 1856. It became a symbol of American independence.

Landscape

Connecticut shares borders with New York, Massachusetts, and Rhode Island. The Connecticut River flows through the center of the state before emptying into Long Island Sound. The name of the river comes from a Native American word meaning "beside the long tidal river," and the state is named after the river. It has a varied landscape, with sandy beaches, forested hills, small towns, and urban areas.

Yale University, in New Haven, is one of Harvard's traditional rivals.

CONNECTICUT FACT FILE

Admitted to Union: 1788 (the 5th state)
Capital: Hartford
Rank in size: 48th
Rank in population: 29th
Nickname: Constitution State

People and Economy

Connecticut's population is densest in the southwest corner of the state, where it is very close to New York City. In recent years the state has seen immigrants arrive from countries such as Guatemala, Laos, Thailand, India, and many others, giving it a diverse population. The state's biggest industry is banking and insurance. Factories throughout the state produce helicopters, jet engines, and submarines, as well as firearms and medicines.

Noah Webster, who created the first American dictionary, was from Connecticut.

The blue waters of the Connecticut River flow through four different states.

RHODE ISLAND

Rhode Island is the smallest state, but it has a rich and varied history. It was founded by Roger Williams (1603–1683) in 1636. He had been banished from Massachusetts because of his religious views, so he bought land from the local tribes to set up a colony where people could worship as they wished. More than a century later, Rhode Island became the first of the 13 colonies to declare its independence from Britain.

The Rhode Island Red breed was developed in Rhode Island. They are known as good egg layers.

Rhode Mainland?

Despite its name, Rhode Island is not an island, although dozens of islands fall within the state's borders. It has several large bays and inlets, including Narragansett Bay, which almost divides the state into two parts. These bays give Rhode Island a long coastline, with many natural harbors and beautiful beaches. During the 19th century, many wealthy families from Boston spent their summers in the seaside town of Newport.

Rhode Island's beautiful coastline makes tourism one of the state's most important industries.

Many Faiths

Rhode Island is very densely populated, with most of the residents living in the main city of Providence. Over the centuries it has had immigrants from many different countries and faiths. The oldest existing Jewish synagogue in the United States is in Newport. More recent immigrants have come from African countries such as Liberia and Ghana.

Rhode Island is a key producer of the hard-shelled clams known as quahogs, which can be made into clam cakes or clam chowder.

RHODE ISLAND FACT FILE

Admitted to Union: 1790 (the 13th state)
Capital: Providence
Rank in size: 50th
Rank in population: 43rd
Nickname: Ocean State

THE MID-ATLANTIC STATES

To the south and west of New England, the mid-Atlantic states stretch down the coast. They include New York, Pennsylvania, New Jersey, Maryland, and Delaware. One historian once called it "the typically American region," but it is hard to define exactly. For example, some people would include Virginia and West Virginia in this region due to their locations, but others would argue that those two states have more in common culturally with the states of the South.

Old and New

In colonial times, the cities of New York and Philadelphia were important centers of trade, culture, and government. At the time, the population ranged from Dutch immigrants in New York to Swedes in Delaware, English settlers in Maryland, and a religious group called the **Quakers** in Pennsylvania. Later, immigrants from Germany, Ireland, Italy, Poland, and elsewhere helped build the region into an industrial powerhouse.

The region's long coastline makes it a popular vacation destination.

Changing Times

Cities such as Buffalo, Newark, and Pittsburgh grew rapidly, and by the turn of the 20th century, New York City was one of the world's major cities. Now, much of the manufacturing has moved elsewhere, but modern industries such as communications have taken over.

HEINZ

Factories such as this one in Pittsburgh, Pennsylvania, helped drive the economy of the mid-Atlantic region.

The mid-Atlantic region is home to many large cities, such as Baltimore, Maryland.

50 STATES FACTS

Throughout its history, the many rivers of the mid-Atlantic states have been put to use as shipping lanes, to transport raw materials and manufactured goods.

NEW YORK

The first European settlers in this region were Dutch fur trappers, who set up trading posts in the early 17th century. Their main town, New Amsterdam, was captured in 1664 by English forces, who renamed it "New York." As a British colony, it was an important source of raw materials such as iron ore, and crops such as wheat. Many of the battles of the Revolutionary War were fought in New York.

Millions of immigrants entered the United States through the processing center on Ellis Island, in New York Harbor.

Land of Contrasts

New York is large and roughly triangle-shaped. In the north are the rugged Adirondack Mountains, and in the southeast is the Hudson River Valley. The large island of Long Island lies off the southern tip of the state. The state has a short Atlantic coastline, but a much longer shoreline to the west and north, where it borders Lake Erie and Lake Ontario.

An International City

Despite its large areas of open land, more than 92 percent of New York's residents live in urban areas, mainly in New York City. This bustling metropolitan area is home to more than 20 million people. More than a third of New Yorkers were born in another country. Outside the cities, there are farms and rural areas.

New York City's mix of immigrants gives it a vibrant culture, with food, music, and art from around the world

The breathtaking Niagara Falls form part of the border between New York and the Canadian province of Ontario.

NEW YORK FACT FILE

Admitted to Union: 1788 (the 11th state)
Capital: Albany
Rank in size: 27th
Rank in population: 3rd
Nickname: Empire State

PENNSYLVANIA

In 1681, King Charles II (1630–1685) of England granted the land that is now Pennsylvania to a man called William Penn (1644–1718). Penn belonged to a religious group called the Quakers, and he offered religious freedom to anyone who lived in the colony. During the Revolutionary War, the Continental Congress met in Philadelphia, and it was there that the Declaration of Independence was signed.

Pennsylvania has more covered wooden bridges than any other state.

Philadelphia was a center of the American Revolution, and it served as the capital of the new nation from 1790 to 1800.

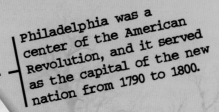

Location, Location, Location

Pennsylvania gets its nickname, "The Keystone State," from its location. It is the dividing point between the Northeast and the South, as well as between the Atlantic and the Midwest regions. The Appalachian Mountains run diagonally through the state, and major rivers such as the Allegheny and Monongahela flow through it. In the southeast, the Delaware River estuary forms a wildlife refuge.

People and Products

Pennsylvania is densely populated, with many people clustered around the cities of Philadelphia in the east and Pittsburgh in the west. The state has a large community of Puerto Rican immigrants, as well as those from China, India, and elsewhere. Pennsylvania's natural resources, especially coal and natural gas, have shaped its history as a center of industry. It is also an important farming state, producing mushrooms, apples, and dairy products.

PENNSYLVANIA FACT FILE

Admitted to Union: 1787 (the 2nd state)
Capital: Harrisburg
Rank in size: 33rd
Rank in population: 6th
Nickname: Keystone State

William Penn died long before the United States became an independent country, but he was made an honorary citizen in 1984.

NEW JERSEY

New Jersey was originally settled by the Dutch, who bought land from the local Lenape tribe. In 1664, it was taken over by the same English fleet that captured New York, and named after the island of Jersey in the English Channel. Many key battles of the Revolutionary War were fought in New Jersey, and the site of George Washington's (1732–1799) military camp is now a national historical park.

George Washington famously crossed the Delaware River near Trenton to launch a surprise attack on the British.

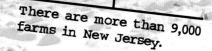

There are more than 9,000 farms in New Jersey.

NEW JERSEY FACT FILE

Admitted to Union: 1787 (the 3rd state)
Capital: Trenton
Rank in size: 47th
Rank in population: 11th
Nickname: Garden State

Bounded by Rivers

The Hudson River separates New Jersey from New York, and the Delaware River forms its border with Pennsylvania. The state has a long Atlantic coastline, with ports, beaches, and tidelands. The northeastern part of the state forms part of the New York City urban area, while other parts are more rural, with forests and mountains.

The container port in Newark is one of the largest in the country.

A Wide Variety

Some people think that New Jersey is little more than a suburb of New York, but there is much more to it than that. The countryside has many small farms, and the state got its nickname of "The Garden State" because of the fruit and vegetables produced there. The Jersey Shore attracts vacationers from all over. The state is incredibly diverse, with residents of Italian-American heritage and immigrants from many countries.

MARYLAND

Many of Maryland's early settlers were Catholics who fled religious persecution in England. In 1814, the brave defense of Fort McHenry against the British inspired the writing of *The Star-Spangled Banner*. Maryland was a slave-owning state, but it did not secede from the **Union** with the other southern states in the 1860s. Many Civil War battles were fought in Maryland, including the bloody Battle of Antietam (1862).

Francis Scott Key wrote the words to the national anthem after witnessing a British attack on Baltimore Harbor.

Split in Half

Maryland has a very short Atlantic coastline, but it is not short on coast! Chesapeake Bay is a large estuary formed where the Susquehanna River and other rivers meet the ocean, and it cuts the state nearly in half. The state's many smaller bays and inlets form an important habitat for a wide variety of plants and animals. The narrow western section of the state, sometimes called the **"panhandle,"** reaches into the Appalachian Mountains.

Nature and Industry

The coast plays an important role in the economy, and Maryland is a big producer of clams, soft-shell crabs, and oysters. However, it is an industrial state as well, with a reputation for cutting-edge scientific research. The busy port of Baltimore handles goods from all over the world, connecting container ships to road and rail transportation.

Assateague Island, which is split between Maryland and Virginia, is home to a famous herd of wild horses.

Chesapeake Bay is the largest estuary in the United States, covering 64,000 square miles.

MARYLAND FACT FILE

Admitted to Union: 1788 (the 7th state)
Capital: Annapolis
Rank in size: 42nd
Rank in population: 19th
Nickname: Old Line State

43

DELAWARE

Early settlements in what is now Delaware were founded by Dutch and Swedish explorers, but in 1664, the English took over. In the early days, Delaware was owned by William Penn, and the colony shared a government with Pennsylvania.

After the Revolutionary War, Delaware was the first state to ratify the new U.S. Constitution, and because of this it is considered to be the first state.

Wilmington is built on the site of Fort Christina, the first Swedish settlement in North America.

The Delaware Memorial Bridge crosses the Delaware River to connect the states of Delaware and New Jersey.

Sea and Land

Delaware shares a long land border with Maryland on the west, and on the east it borders Delaware Bay and the Atlantic Ocean. Most of the land in the state is low and flat, with rich soil. It has the lowest average **elevation** of any state, but in the northern part there are rolling hills. About two-thirds of the state's population live in Wilmington, the largest city.

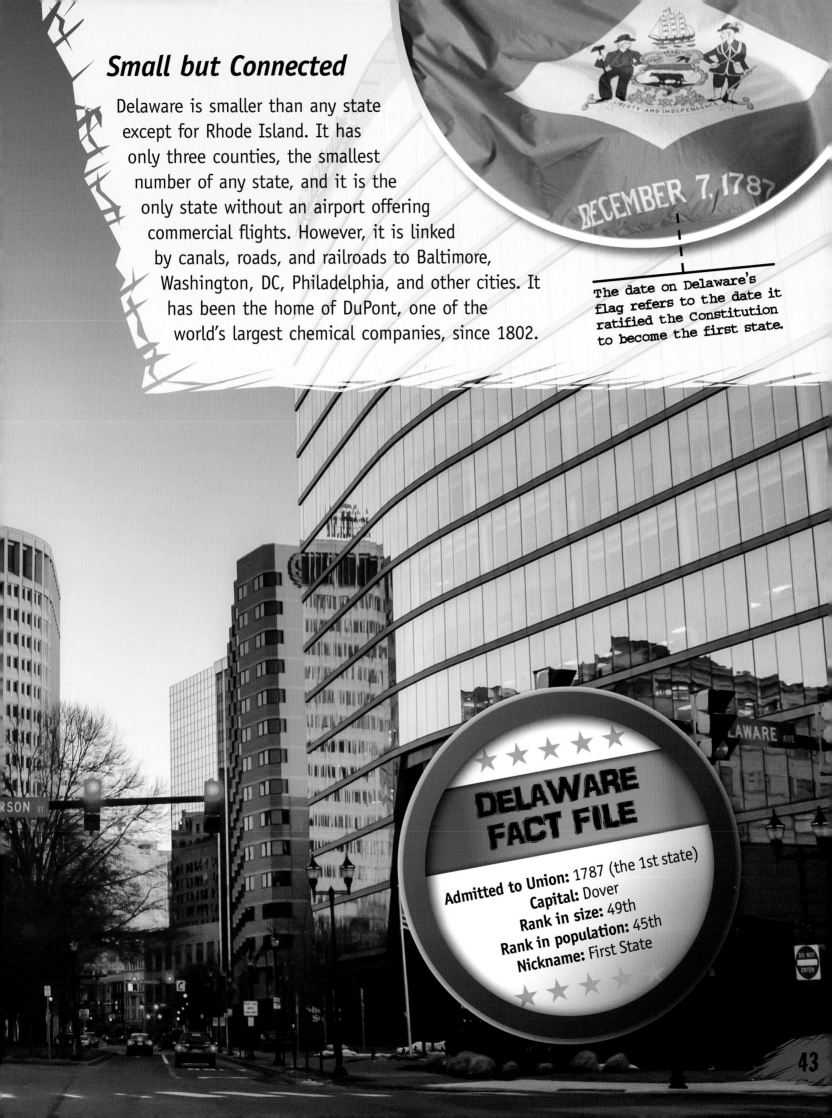

Small but Connected

Delaware is smaller than any state except for Rhode Island. It has only three counties, the smallest number of any state, and it is the only state without an airport offering commercial flights. However, it is linked by canals, roads, and railroads to Baltimore, Washington, DC, Philadelphia, and other cities. It has been the home of DuPont, one of the world's largest chemical companies, since 1802.

DECEMBER 7, 1787

The date on Delaware's flag refers to the date it ratified the Constitution to become the first state.

DELAWARE FACT FILE

Admitted to Union: 1787 (the 1st state)
Capital: Dover
Rank in size: 49th
Rank in population: 45th
Nickname: First State

THE SOUTHEAST

Before Europeans arrived, the southeastern part of the country was home to Native American groups such as the Seminole, Choctaw, Creek, Cherokee, and Chickasaw. Spanish and French explorers started settlements in Florida, including St. Augustine, the oldest continuously inhabited European settlement in the United States. Four of the states—Virginia, North and South Carolina, and Georgia—were part of the original 13 colonies.

The Appalachian Mountains run through many of the states of the Southeast.

The fort built by the Spanish in St. Augustine, Florida, is still standing.

The Civil War

Before the Civil War, slavery was allowed in the Southern states but not in the North. Disagreements arose about the federal government's right to outlaw slavery in territories that were not yet states. Between December 1860 and June 1861, 11 of the slave states seceded from the Union. This led to the Civil War, the bloodiest conflict in the nation's history. After the war, the Southern states rejoined the Union.

Stone Mountain in Georgia has carvings showing leaders of the **Confederacy**.

Vibrant Culture

Today, the Southeast, which includes Virginia, West Virginia, North and South Carolina, Georgia, Florida, Alabama, Mississippi, Tennessee, Kentucky, Arkansas, and Louisiana, is proud of its unique customs, food, and music, as well as its reputation for "Southern hospitality." The population is a mix of descendants of the Native Americans who originally lived there, the Europeans who colonized it, and the African slaves who were forced to work the land. More recently, immigrants have arrived from Cuba, Puerto Rico, and elsewhere.

In the past, large farms called plantations dominated the Southeast, and farming is still important.

50 STATES FACTS

There is a wide range of different **dialects** and accents found in the Southeast. Some, like Gullah, have African roots, and others, such as Cajun, date back to French settlements.

45

VIRGINIA

Few states have played as large a role in U.S. history as Virginia. It was the site of Jamestown, the first permanent English colony in the United States. Eight presidents, including George Washington and Thomas Jefferson, were born here. The state was the site of the Battle of Yorktown (1781), where the British Army surrendered to end the Revolutionary War, as well as several important Civil War battles.

Thomas Jefferson's home, Monticello, is preserved as a museum.

Shrinking State

Before the Civil War, Virginia included the land that is now the state of West Virginia. Now, even without that region, the state still has a varied landscape. In the east, it borders the Atlantic Ocean and Chesapeake Bay. To the west, a coastal plain stretches toward the **Piedmont**, where the land begins to rise. The beautiful Blue Ridge Mountains and other Appalachian peaks lie in the western part of the state. Government buildings such as the Pentagon are found in the northeast, near the border with Washington, DC.

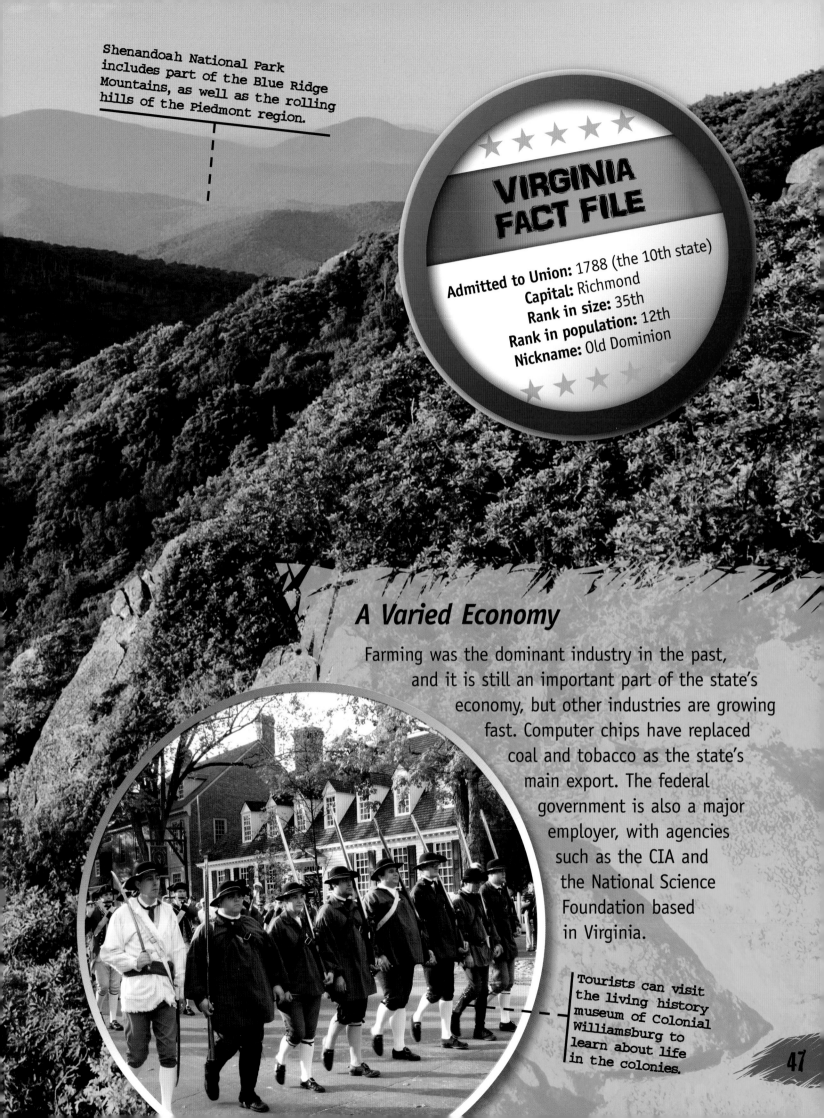

Shenandoah National Park includes part of the Blue Ridge Mountains, as well as the rolling hills of the Piedmont region.

VIRGINIA FACT FILE

Admitted to Union: 1788 (the 10th state)
Capital: Richmond
Rank in size: 35th
Rank in population: 12th
Nickname: Old Dominion

A Varied Economy

Farming was the dominant industry in the past, and it is still an important part of the state's economy, but other industries are growing fast. Computer chips have replaced coal and tobacco as the state's main export. The federal government is also a major employer, with agencies such as the CIA and the National Science Foundation based in Virginia.

Tourists can visit the living history museum of Colonial Williamsburg to learn about life in the colonies.

47

WEST VIRGINIA

West Virginia is the youngest state in the Southeast. It was part of Virginia until the Civil War, but when Virginia seceded to join the Confederacy in 1861, residents of its western counties did not want to join them. Instead, they seceded from the rest of the state and sided with the Union. West Virginia was admitted as a state in 1863.

President Abraham Lincoln (1809–1865) signed the order proclaiming West Virginia as a state in 1863.

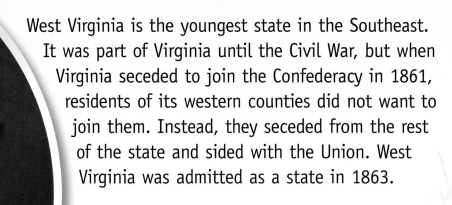

The Mountain State

West Virginia is unique among the states for its entire area falling within a mountain range. The Appalachians cover the state from one end to the other, giving it the highest average elevation of any state east of the Mississippi River. Thick forests cover the terrain of large portions of the state, and it has many rivers. The Ohio River forms a long border between West Virginia and Ohio.

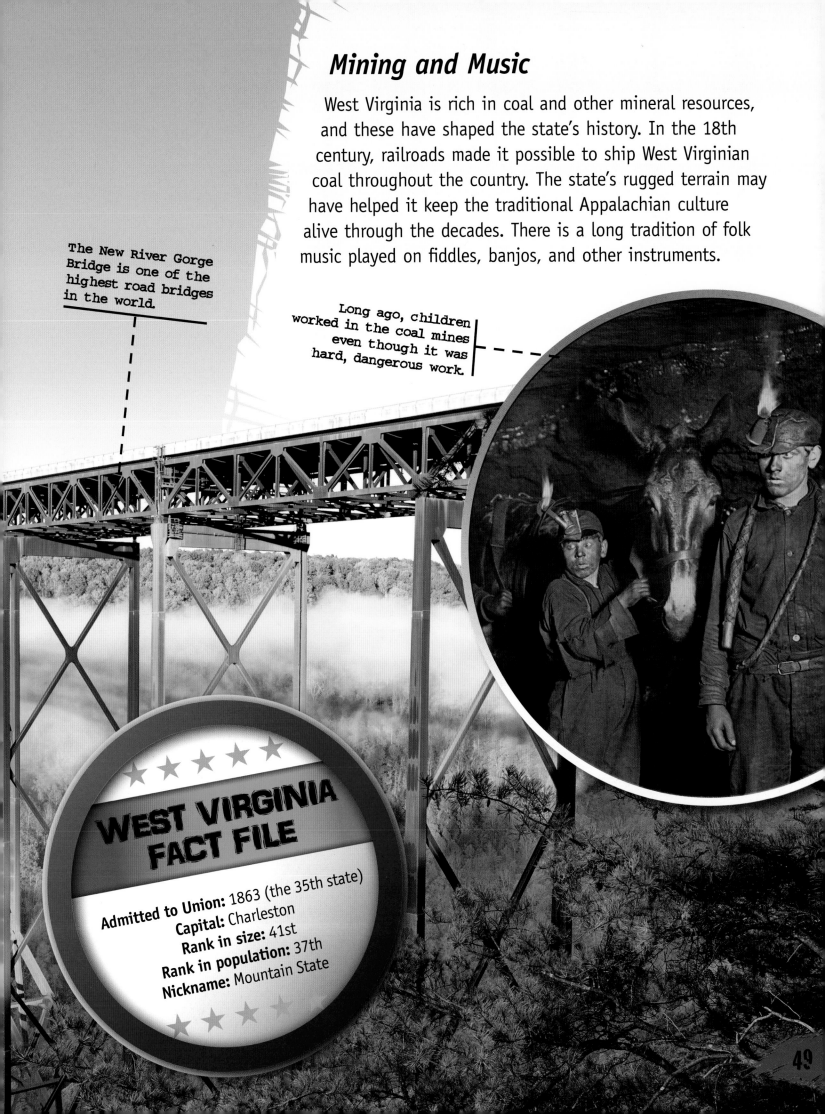

Mining and Music

West Virginia is rich in coal and other mineral resources, and these have shaped the state's history. In the 18th century, railroads made it possible to ship West Virginian coal throughout the country. The state's rugged terrain may have helped it keep the traditional Appalachian culture alive through the decades. There is a long tradition of folk music played on fiddles, banjos, and other instruments.

The New River Gorge Bridge is one of the highest road bridges in the world.

Long ago, children worked in the coal mines even though it was hard, dangerous work.

WEST VIRGINIA FACT FILE

Admitted to Union: 1863 (the 35th state)
Capital: Charleston
Rank in size: 41st
Rank in population: 37th
Nickname: Mountain State

NORTH CAROLINA

In 1585, a group of English settlers established a colony on Roanoke Island, off the coast of what is now North Carolina. Although it did not last, this village was the first English settlement in what is now the United States. North Carolina was one of the first 13 colonies, and it joined the Confederacy during the Civil War.

The first ever airplane flight was made by the Wright brothers at Kitty Hawk, North Carolina, in 1903.

NORTH CAROLINA FACT FILE

Admitted to Union: 1789 (the 12th state)
Capital: Raleigh
Rank in size: 28th
Rank in population: 10th
Nickname: Tar Heel State

Old and New

North Carolina's rich history means that it is full of historic towns, battlefields, and quaint villages, but this is only part of the picture. It is also the home of modern cities such as Charlotte, as well as universities and high-tech research facilities. Agriculture and manufacturing are important, and the state is a leading producer of tobacco, textiles, and furniture.

North Carolina's Outer Banks are a popular vacation destination.

Coast and Mountains

The eastern half of the state is made up of a broad coastal plain, and in the west are the Appalachian Mountains, with a region of rolling foothills between the two. The Atlantic Coast is fringed with a string of narrow, sandy **barrier islands** called the Outer Banks. On one of the islands is Cape Hatteras. So many ships have been lost in the waters off Cape Hatteras that it is known as "the graveyard of the Atlantic."

The insect-eating Venus flytrap plant is native to North Carolina.

SOUTH CAROLINA

In the 16th century, Spanish and French explorers arrived in the land that is now South Carolina to find many small tribes of Native Americans. It was only in 1670 that a permanent English settlement was set up. Over the years, hundreds of thousands of slaves were brought to South Carolina to work on the plantations. Many battles of the Revolutionary War were fought here, and it became the eighth state in 1788.

There are many historic buildings in the section of Charleston known as the "French Quarter."

Up Country and Low Country

South Carolina is shaped like a triangle and has two main geographic regions. Along the Atlantic Coast, the Low Country is home to sandy beaches, cypress swamps, and historic ports such as Georgetown and Charleston. To the northwest, the Piedmont **plateau** rises until it reaches the Blue Ridge Mountains at the far northwest corner of the state. The climate is generally hot and humid.

The remains of Fort Sumter, where the first battle of the Civil War was fought, can still be seen.

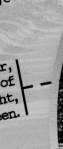

Beaches and Plantations

In the early days, South Carolina became rich as a center of agriculture and trade. Huge plantations produced rice, indigo, and cotton, but they depended on the labor of African slaves.

Today the state is still an important producer of cotton, lumber, tobacco, and soybeans, as well as manufacturing textiles, chemicals, and machinery. Tourists also come to the state to take advantage of the beautiful beaches and historic sites.

SOUTH CAROLINA FACT FILE

Admitted to Union: 1788 (the 8th state)
Capital: Columbia
Rank in size: 40th
Rank in population: 24th
Nickname: Palmetto State

South Carolina's wild areas include several cypress swamps.

Rows of stately live oaks line the drives of many plantations.

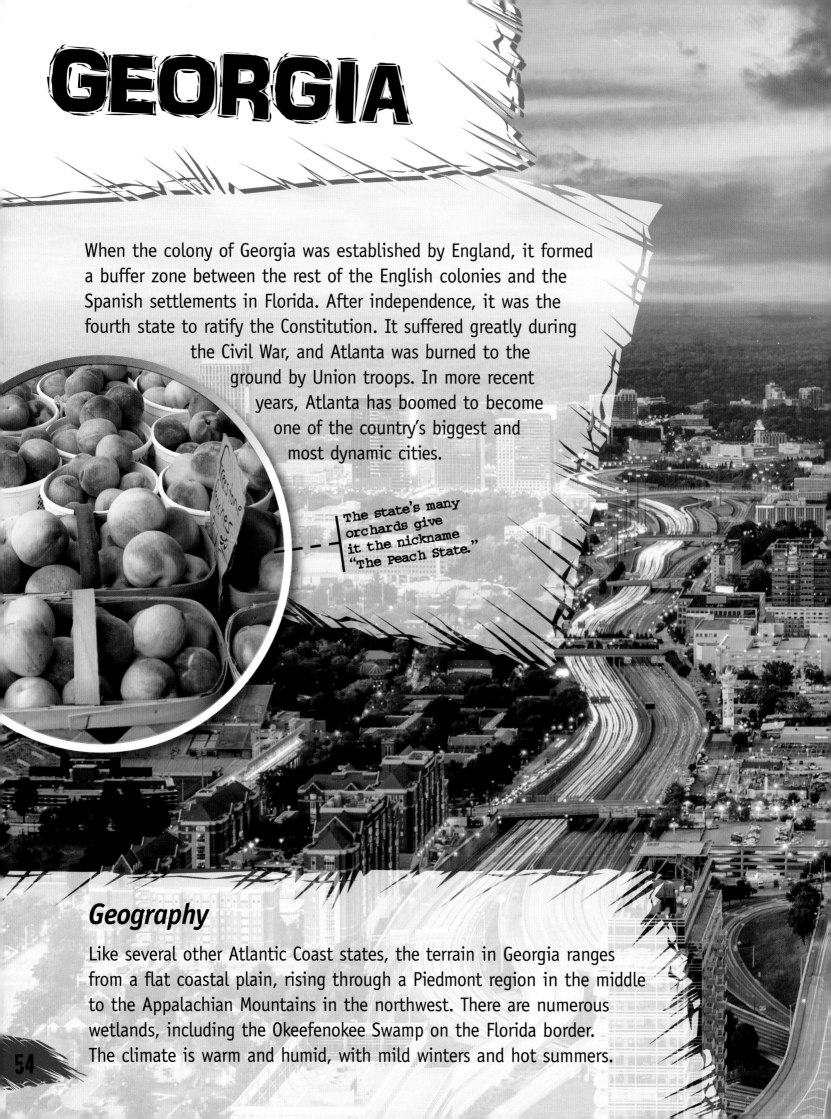

GEORGIA

When the colony of Georgia was established by England, it formed a buffer zone between the rest of the English colonies and the Spanish settlements in Florida. After independence, it was the fourth state to ratify the Constitution. It suffered greatly during the Civil War, and Atlanta was burned to the ground by Union troops. In more recent years, Atlanta has boomed to become one of the country's biggest and most dynamic cities.

The state's many orchards give it the nickname "The Peach State."

Geography

Like several other Atlantic Coast states, the terrain in Georgia ranges from a flat coastal plain, rising through a Piedmont region in the middle to the Appalachian Mountains in the northwest. There are numerous wetlands, including the Okeefenokee Swamp on the Florida border. The climate is warm and humid, with mild winters and hot summers.

Cotton and Stone

Georgia's history was built on cotton, and agriculture is still important. It is the country's largest producer of peanuts, and it is famous for growing tobacco, pecans, and peaches. There are quarries where marble is produced, and marble from Georgia was used to build the Lincoln Memorial in Washington, DC. The state has also produced many famous authors and musicians.

Atlanta is a bustling city, with the world's busiest airport.

In the 18th century, almost all flat, rich soil in Georgia was planted with cotton. It is still a major crop today.

GEORGIA FACT FILE

Admitted to Union: 1788 (the 4th state)
Capital: Atlanta
Rank in size: 24th
Rank in population: 9th
Nickname: Peach State

FLORIDA

Florida became the first state to be visited by Europeans when the Spanish explorer Juan Ponce de León (1474–1521) landed there in 1513. The British forced the Spanish out in 1763, but after the Revolutionary War, the colony—which had stayed loyal to the British—was given back to Spain. In 1821, they passed it on to the United States, and Florida became a state in 1845.

Everglades National Park preserves some of the state's unique wetlands.

Warm and Beautiful

Florida's mild climate, sandy beaches, and unusual plants and animals have attracted people to the state for many years. Most of the state is at or near sea level, with huge areas of wetlands. From the southern tip of the state, the Florida Keys stretch out into the Gulf of Mexico. Florida deserves its nickname of "The Sunshine State," but it is also hit by thunderstorms and **hurricanes**.

Florida has more than 600 miles of beaches.

A Destination State

Tourism is one of the state's main industries. Not only do many people come to visit the beaches, theme parks, and natural wonders, but some also choose to retire here. The state is famous for its oranges, but tomatoes, sugar cane, and grapefruit are also important crops. Immigrants from Cuba, Puerto Rico, and elsewhere have given the state a rich culture.

Florida's coast is home to Kennedy Space Center, NASA's base for launching rockets and other spacecraft.

FLORIDA FACT FILE

Admitted to Union: 1845 (the 27th state)
Capital: Tallahassee
Rank in size: 22nd
Rank in population: 4th
Nickname: Sunshine State

ALABAMA

Spanish explorers were the first Europeans to pass through Alabama, and it was a French colony for many years. After the Revolutionary War, it was divided between the United States and Spain. It finally became a state in 1819. During the Civil War, its capital city, Montgomery, served as the capital of the Confederacy. Many key events in the **civil rights movement** of the 1960s took place in Alabama.

Martin Luther King Jr. lived in Montgomery and helped to organize the civil rights movement.

ALABAMA FACT FILE

Admitted to Union: 1819 (the 22nd state)
Capital: Montgomery
Rank in size: 30th
Rank in population: 23rd
Nickname: Heart of Dixie

Rockets and Writers

Farming is important in Alabama, and major products include cotton, corn, chicken, and cattle. Manufacturing is even more important to the state's economy, and Huntsville is the center for much of the United States' research into rockets and other spacecraft. Alabama is famous for its country and blues music, and it has been the home of authors such as Zora Neale Hurston (1891–1960) and Harper Lee (1926–2016).

Alabama's rivers are one of its most important natural resources.

Many of NASA's rockets and spacecraft are designed in Huntsville.

Coast and Waterways

Alabama is bordered by Mississippi to the west, Tennessee to the north, Georgia to the east, and Florida to the south. It has a short coastline along the Gulf of Mexico, where the city of Mobile serves as a major seaport. Alabama's network of rivers, lakes, and wetlands supports a wide variety of wildlife, and also makes water transportation an important industry.

MISSISSIPPI

Mississippi shares its name with a Native American mound-building civilization that was there long before European explorers arrived. It was ruled at different times by the Spanish, the French, and the British, then became a territory of the United States after the Revolutionary War. It joined the Confederacy during the Civil War, and was a center of the civil rights movement.

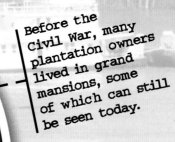

Before the Civil War, many plantation owners lived in grand mansions, some of which can still be seen today.

Cotton and Art

In the past, Mississippi's economy was based on cotton plantations worked by huge numbers of slaves. In the decades after the Civil War, hundreds of thousands of African-Americans left the state to find jobs in the North. Even so, Mississippi still has the highest percentage of African-Americans of any state. Like its neighbor, Alabama, Mississippi has produced many great writers and musicians, including William Faulkner (1897–1962), Tennessee Williams (1911–1983), B.B. King (1925–2015), and Elvis Presley (1935–1977).

Barges of goods are still shipped down the Mississippi River.

MISSISSIPPI FACT FILE

Admitted to Union: 1817 (the 20th state)
Capital: Jackson
Rank in size: 32nd
Rank in population: 31st
Nickname: Magnolia State

A River State

In shape, Mississippi is almost a mirror image of its neighbor to the east, Alabama. The Mississippi River forms the western border of the state, and it has a short coastline on the Gulf of Mexico. The state has low hills but no mountains, and much of it is part of the vast Mississippi **Delta**. Farms, forests, and wetlands cover much of the land.

Catfish farming is a major industry in Mississippi. It is the largest producer in the United States.

61

TENNESSEE

The Appalachian Mountains separate the land that is now Tennessee from the 13 original colonies. For the early settlers, Tennessee was a wild **frontier** land. Small bands of traveling hunters were followed by those who built homes, and the region became a state in 1796. Tennessee joined the Confederacy during the Civil War. In 1920, it ratified the 19th **Amendment**, giving the amendment approval from enough states to grant women across the country the right to vote.

Early settlers in Tennessee often built log cabins.

Divided in Three

Tennessee is one of only two states to border eight other states: Kentucky, Virginia, North Carolina, Georgia, Alabama, Mississippi, Arkansas, and Missouri. The eastern part of the state is mountainous, and the central part is marked by rolling hills and rich valleys. The Mississippi River forms the western border of the state, and this part of the state has mainly low, flat land.

TENNESSEE FACT FILE

Admitted to Union: 1796 (the 16th state)
Capital: Nashville
Rank in size: 36th
Rank in population: 17th
Nickname: Volunteer State

62

Music and Power

Tennessee is probably most famous for its music. People come to Nashville from all over the country to play and listen to country and rockabilly music. A major blues and rock scene is centered in Memphis. Aside from music, farming and manufacturing are also important. The state's many rivers and dams help it generate hydroelectric power on a large scale.

Many famous country musicians started their careers in the music venues of Nashville.

The Great Smoky Mountains National Park is the most visited national park in the United States.

Norris Dam was built in the 1930s and still produces hydroelectricity.

KENTUCKY

In the 1770s, settlers began to move into Kentucky from Virginia, North Carolina, and Pennsylvania. They arranged to buy land from the local Cherokee people, and more settlers arrived as the Revolutionary War dragged on. Kentucky was admitted to the Union as a slave state, but it did not join the Confederacy during the Civil War. Its residents were deeply divided about which side to support.

Goldenrod is the state flower of Kentucky.

A River State

Kentucky's borders are formed by the Ohio River in the north and the Mississippi River in the west. The state's many rivers and lakes give it more miles of waterways than most other states. There are mountains in the east, vast rolling fields of bluegrass in the center, and floodplains and swamps in the west. The state is also home to Mammoth Cave, the longest known cave system in the world.

Mammoth Cave has been preserved as a national park since 1941.

The white fences of horse farms are a common sight in the Kentucky countryside.

Horses and Music

Outside of Lexington and Louisville, Kentucky is mainly rural, and it is famous as a center of horse breeding. The country's most important horse race, the Kentucky Derby, is held in Louisville every May. The state is also known as the main producer of bourbon whiskey. Kentucky's rich musical heritage includes Appalachian folk music and bluegrass.

KENTUCKY FACT FILE

Admitted to Union: 1792 (the 15th state)
Capital: Frankfort
Rank in size: 37th
Rank in population: 26th
Nickname: Bluegrass State

ARKANSAS

The region that is now Arkansas was explored by people from France and Spain. In 1803, it was bought by the United States as part of the Louisiana Purchase. After a long debate, slavery was allowed in the Arkansas Territory, but slave-owning was mostly limited to the cotton plantations in the Southeast. Arkansas became part of the Confederacy during the Civil War.

The city of Hot Springs has many bathhouses where people could enjoy the natural hot springs.

Mountains and Springs

Arkansas is known as "The Natural State," and it is easy to see why. The Ozark and the Ouachita Mountains are found in the northwest, and the southeast is mainly lowlands. The state has many rivers and lakes, as well as caves and natural hot springs. Many people come to the state to travel on the rivers, hike through the forests and mountains, and soak in the hot springs.

Arkansas's beautiful scenery is one of its biggest draws.

Crops and Crafts

Arkansas's dense forests supply the lumber and paper industries that are an important part of the state's economy. However, farming still dominates many parts of the state. Farms raise cattle, chickens, and hogs, and grow soybeans and cotton. Arkansas is the country's largest producer of rice, producing nearly half of all rice grown in the United States. The state is also known for crafts such as basket weaving, quilting, and woodturning.

Rice has been grown in Arkansas for more than 100 years.

ARKANSAS FACT FILE

Admitted to Union: 1836 (the 25th state)
Capital: Little Rock
Rank in size: 29th
Rank in population: 32nd
Nickname: Natural State

LOUISIANA

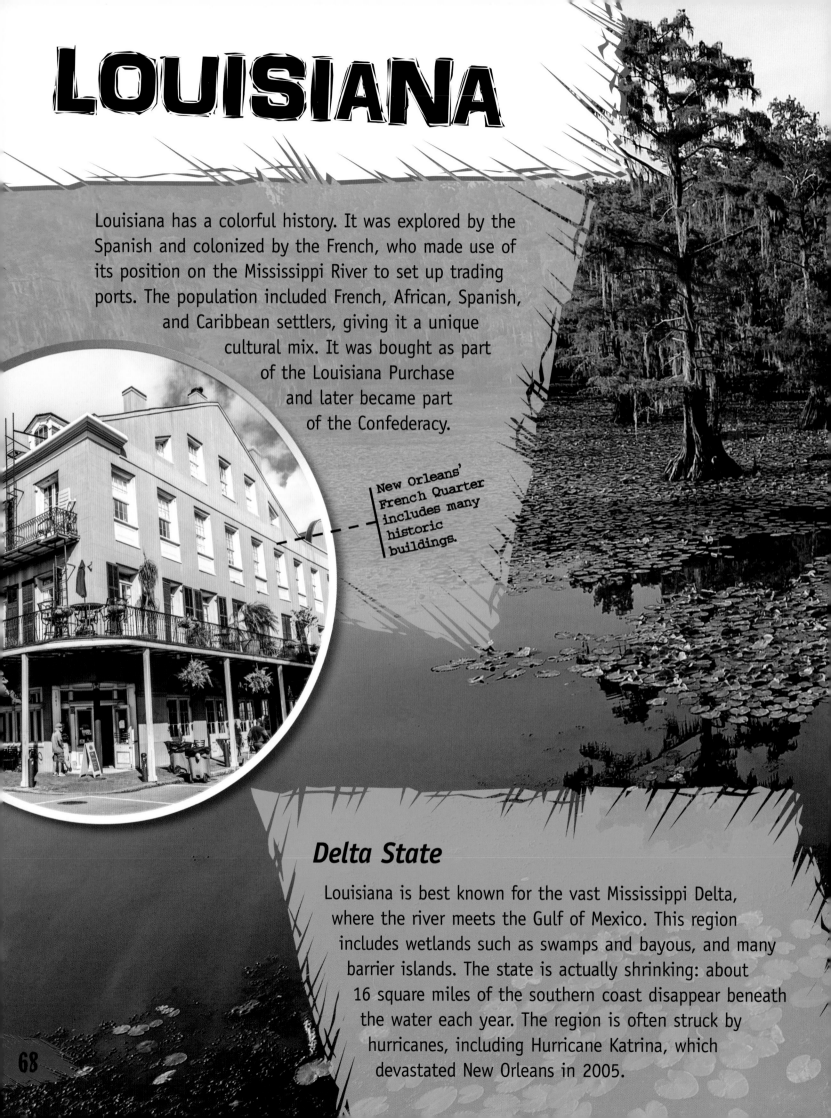

Louisiana has a colorful history. It was explored by the Spanish and colonized by the French, who made use of its position on the Mississippi River to set up trading ports. The population included French, African, Spanish, and Caribbean settlers, giving it a unique cultural mix. It was bought as part of the Louisiana Purchase and later became part of the Confederacy.

New Orleans' French Quarter includes many historic buildings.

Delta State

Louisiana is best known for the vast Mississippi Delta, where the river meets the Gulf of Mexico. This region includes wetlands such as swamps and bayous, and many barrier islands. The state is actually shrinking: about 16 square miles of the southern coast disappear beneath the water each year. The region is often struck by hurricanes, including Hurricane Katrina, which devastated New Orleans in 2005.

Louisiana's wetlands form an important habitat for many different plants and animals, including alligators.

Shipping and Jazz

Louisiana is still important as a transportation hub. Goods are brought by rail to ports in New Orleans and Baton Rouge, before being loaded onto ships to be sent to the rest of the world. The state is also known for oil and gas extraction, and it is the world's largest producer of crawfish. Tourists flock to New Orleans to enjoy its distinctive history, Cajun culture, and jazz music.

New Orleans is famous for a style of jazz called Dixieland.

LOUISIANA FACT FILE

Admitted to Union: 1812 (the 18th state)
Capital: Baton Rouge
Rank in size: 31st
Rank in population: 25th
Nickname: Pelican State

THE MIDWEST

The region known as the Midwest was seen as a land of opportunity by many settlers during the country's early history. Families moved west in search of land where they could carve out a living for themselves. One by one, new states were created out of this wild territory. Now the region is a center of manufacturing as well as farming. The Midwest includes Ohio, Michigan, Indiana, Illinois, Wisconsin, Minnesota, Iowa, Missouri, Kansas, Nebraska, and North and South Dakota.

50 STATES FACT

The "Midwestern accent" is the one you are most likely to hear on national newscasts. As a result, many Midwesterners say that they speak without an accent.

Some cities of the Midwest are known for blues and jazz music.

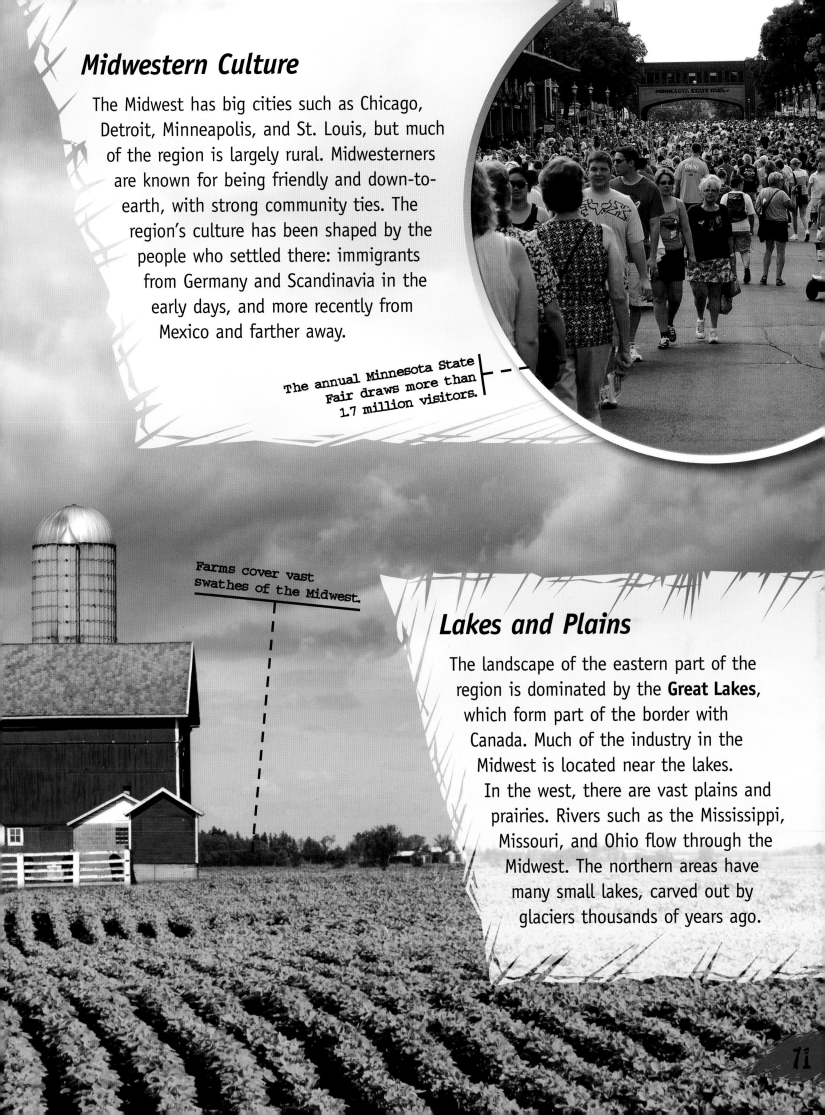

Midwestern Culture

The Midwest has big cities such as Chicago, Detroit, Minneapolis, and St. Louis, but much of the region is largely rural. Midwesterners are known for being friendly and down-to-earth, with strong community ties. The region's culture has been shaped by the people who settled there: immigrants from Germany and Scandinavia in the early days, and more recently from Mexico and farther away.

The annual Minnesota State Fair draws more than 1.7 million visitors.

Farms cover vast swathes of the Midwest.

Lakes and Plains

The landscape of the eastern part of the region is dominated by the **Great Lakes**, which form part of the border with Canada. Much of the industry in the Midwest is located near the lakes.

In the west, there are vast plains and prairies. Rivers such as the Mississippi, Missouri, and Ohio flow through the Midwest. The northern areas have many small lakes, carved out by glaciers thousands of years ago.

OHIO

In the 18th century, French fur trappers founded trading posts in the land that is now Ohio. After the Revolutionary War, the new U.S. government set up the Northwest Territory. It covered the region west of the Appalachians, bordered by Canada and the Great Lakes to the north, the Ohio River to the south, and the Mississippi River to the west. In 1803, Ohio became the first state to be founded from this territory.

Cleveland was the first city in the United States to be lit by electricity.

A Gateway State

Ohio's location has meant that for many years, its roads, railroads, and canals have linked the western part of the country with the northeast. It has a long border along Lake Erie to the north, and the Ohio River forms its southern border with Kentucky and West Virginia. Most of the state is fairly flat, but there are rugged hills in the southeast, near the border with West Virginia.

For many years, Ohio led the nation in producing rubber for tires and other uses.

City and Country

Ohio is a mix of urban and rural. In the rural areas, the landscape is dotted with farms and small towns. Big industrial cities such as Cleveland, Cincinnati, and Akron produce goods to ship around the world. Many people from Ohio have shaped the country's history, from the Wright Brothers and the astronauts John Glenn (born 1921) and Neil Armstrong (1930–2012), to the eight presidents who have called Ohio home.

Neil Armstrong, the first man to walk on the moon, is one of the most famous Ohioans.

OHIO FACT FILE

Admitted to Union: 1803 (the 17th state)
Capital: Columbus
Rank in size: 34th
Rank in population: 7th
Nickname: Buckeye State

MICHIGAN

The land that is now Michigan was once home to many Native Americans of the Algonquian group. French explorers and trappers started to settle in Michigan in the 17th century, and in 1701, they founded the city of Detroit. The land then passed to the British, and later to the newly formed United States. Michigan became a state in 1837. In the 20th century, it was transformed by the growth of the automobile industry.

The river that runs through Detroit forms a border between the United States and Canada.

MICHIGAN FACT FILE

Admitted to Union: 1837 (the 26th state)
Capital: Lansing
Rank in size: 11th
Rank in population: 8th
Nickname: Great Lakes State

The Mackinac Bridge connects the Upper and Lower Peninsulas of Michigan.

Diana Ross, born and raised in Detroit, was one of the stars of the Motown scene.

Motown, Motors, and More

Michigan's famous automobile industry has faced challenges in the last few decades, but the state is starting to recover, and Michigan can boast other important industries. Motown, one of the most famous recording companies in the world, has its roots there, and Battle Creek is the home of Kellogg's, making it the cereal capital of the world! With the Erie Canal and intersection of railroads, Michigan continues to be a center for transporting goods across America.

Two Peninsulas

Michigan is made up of two peninsulas: the Lower Peninsula, which shares a southern border with Indiana and Ohio, and the Upper Peninsula. The two parts of the state are separated by the Straits of Mackinac. Michigan is bordered by four of the five Great Lakes, giving it the longest freshwater coastline in the United States.

INDIANA

Indiana gets its name from the many Native Americans who used to live there. However, after battles with European settlers, many of them fled to Canada or west of the Mississippi River. Indiana was part of the Northwest Territory before becoming a state in 1816. Settlers came to Indiana from the eastern states, some traveling by steamboat along the Ohio River.

The cardinal is the state bird of Indiana.

Indiana is bordered by Lake Michigan, where you can see the beautiful Indiana Dunes.

Central City

Indiana has one large city: its capital, Indianapolis, which is located in the center of the state. Outside of the city, the state is largely rural, with smaller towns and many farms. The north and central portions of Indiana are fairly flat, while the south is hillier. There are many state parks, forests, and nature reserves, and vacationers come to Indiana for activities such as fishing, hiking, and camping.

Indianapolis has many museums, theaters, and historic sites.

Corn and Cars

Factories in northern Indiana produce steel and chemicals, as well as industrial machinery and heavy equipment. Farms in other parts of the state produce corn, which is used to feed pigs and cattle. There are also vineyards and wineries in the southeast. Indiana is the home of the Indianapolis Motor Speedway, which hosts the famous Indy 500 auto race every May.

The NASCAR Brickyard 400 race is held at the Indianapolis Motor Speedway.

INDIANA FACT FILE

Admitted to Union: 1816 (the 19th state)
Capital: Indianapolis
Rank in size: 38th
Rank in population: 15th
Nickname: Hoosier State

ILLINOIS

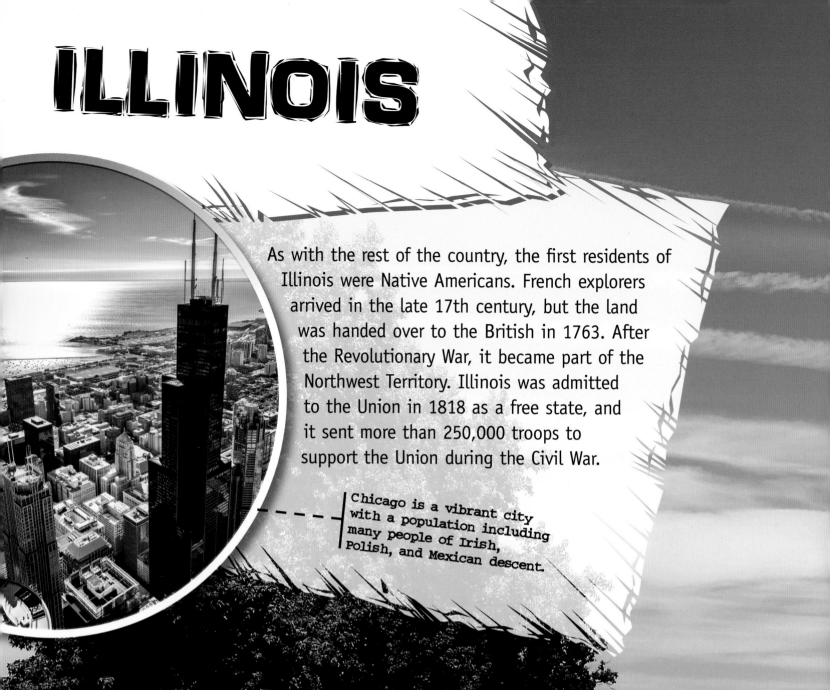

As with the rest of the country, the first residents of Illinois were Native Americans. French explorers arrived in the late 17th century, but the land was handed over to the British in 1763. After the Revolutionary War, it became part of the Northwest Territory. Illinois was admitted to the Union in 1818 as a free state, and it sent more than 250,000 troops to support the Union during the Civil War.

Chicago is a vibrant city with a population including many people of Irish, Polish, and Mexican descent.

City and Country

The city of Chicago is at the northeast corner of Illinois, where it has a shoreline along Lake Michigan. This part of the state is dominated by the sprawling city and its suburbs. The central part of Illinois is mainly prairie, with small towns and farms. The southern part of the state, sometimes known as "Little Egypt," has more hills and a large national forest.

Feeding the World

Chicago, the third-largest city in the United States, is the cultural and economic heart of the state. It is a major transportation hub, and also has many factories and businesses. In the past, it was a center of the meatpacking industry, and food processing is still important there. The farms that fill much of the rest of the state produce soybeans, corn, and fruit.

Illinois is one of the biggest soybean-producing states in the country.

Cahokia Mounds, in the southern part of the state, were built by Native Americans hundreds of years ago.

ILLINOIS FACT FILE

Admitted to Union: 1818 (the 21st state)
Capital: Springfield
Rank in size: 25th
Rank in population: 5th
Nickname: Prairie State

WISCONSIN

The Wisconsin Dells, a long gorge on the Wisconsin River, has many beautiful rock formations.

Wisconsin was inhabited by Native Americans when the French explorer Jean Nicolet (1598–1642) opened a trading post in 1634. Fur trapping was replaced by lead mining when the area became part of the Northwest Territory. The lead miners, who sometimes lived in the tunnels they dug, were known as "badgers," giving the state its nickname. German immigrants flocked to the new state, setting up small farms.

The badger is the state animal of Wisconsin.

Rivers and Hills

Wisconsin has a long border with Lake Michigan on the east, and the Mississippi River runs along the western part of the state. The northern part of the state has forests, lakes, and hills. There are plains in the central section, and in the southwest is a hilly region with many rivers and streams. Many of the state's cities, such as Milwaukee and Madison, are in the southeast.

America's Dairyland

After Wisconsin became a state, farming began to take
over from lead mining. The state is now the country's
leading producer of cheese, and it is near the top for
milk and butter. Many Wisconsin residents proudly call
themselves "cheeseheads." The state is also known
for its beer and bratwurst, and tourists
come to enjoy the region's rivers,
lakes, and beautiful scenery.

Wisconsin has over
12 million cows,
producing more than
3.2 billion gallons of
milk each year.

WISCONSIN FACT FILE

Admitted to Union: 1848 (the 30th state)
Capital: Madison
Rank in size: 23rd
Rank in population: 20th
Nickname: Badger State

MINNESOTA

Some of the land that is now Minnesota joined the United States as part of the Louisiana Purchase in 1803. When European settlers moved into the state, they often came into conflict with the native Dakota people. This led to the short Dakota War of 1862, after which the remaining Native Americans were forced out. Immigrants from Scandinavia and Germany helped build the state's thriving economy.

Minneapolis's Skyway system of pedestrian bridges allows people to move from one building to another without having to go outside.

MINNESOTA FACT FILE

Admitted to Union: 1858 (the 32nd state)
Capital: St. Paul
Rank in size: 12th
Rank in population: 21st
Nickname: North Star State

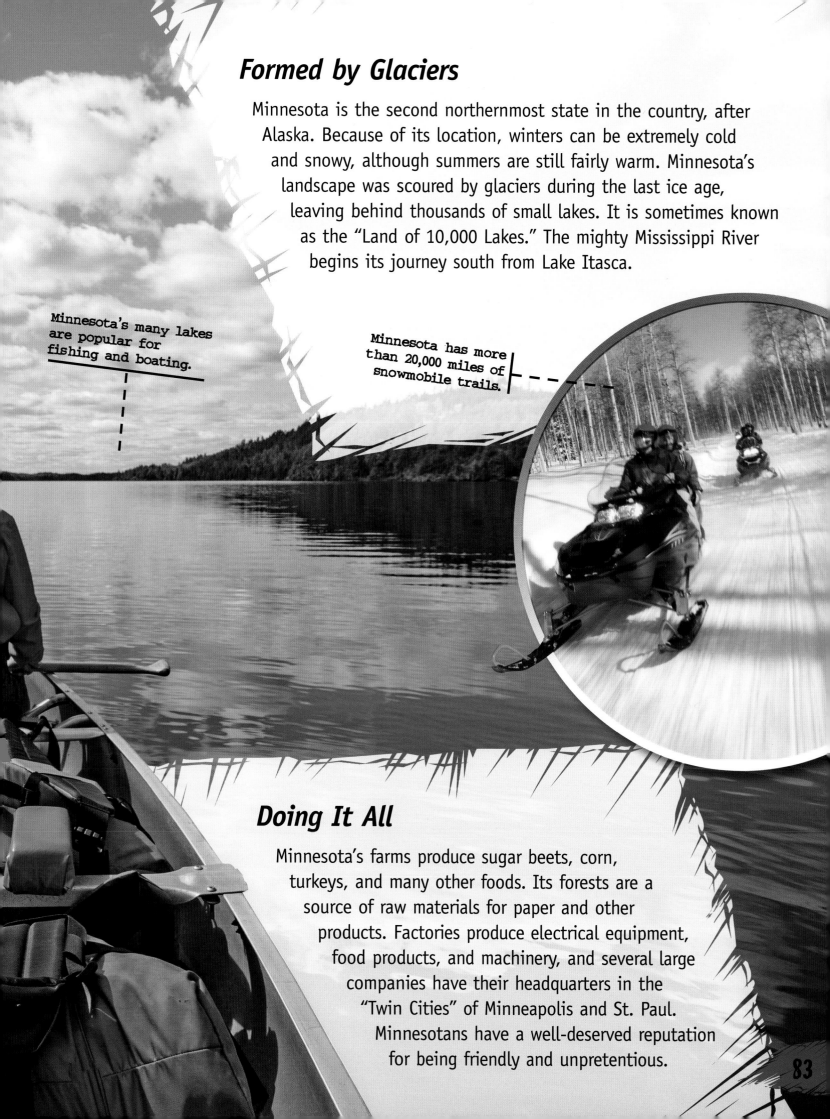

Formed by Glaciers

Minnesota is the second northernmost state in the country, after Alaska. Because of its location, winters can be extremely cold and snowy, although summers are still fairly warm. Minnesota's landscape was scoured by glaciers during the last ice age, leaving behind thousands of small lakes. It is sometimes known as the "Land of 10,000 Lakes." The mighty Mississippi River begins its journey south from Lake Itasca.

Minnesota's many lakes are popular for fishing and boating.

Minnesota has more than 20,000 miles of snowmobile trails.

Doing It All

Minnesota's farms produce sugar beets, corn, turkeys, and many other foods. Its forests are a source of raw materials for paper and other products. Factories produce electrical equipment, food products, and machinery, and several large companies have their headquarters in the "Twin Cities" of Minneapolis and St. Paul. Minnesotans have a well-deserved reputation for being friendly and unpretentious.

IOWA

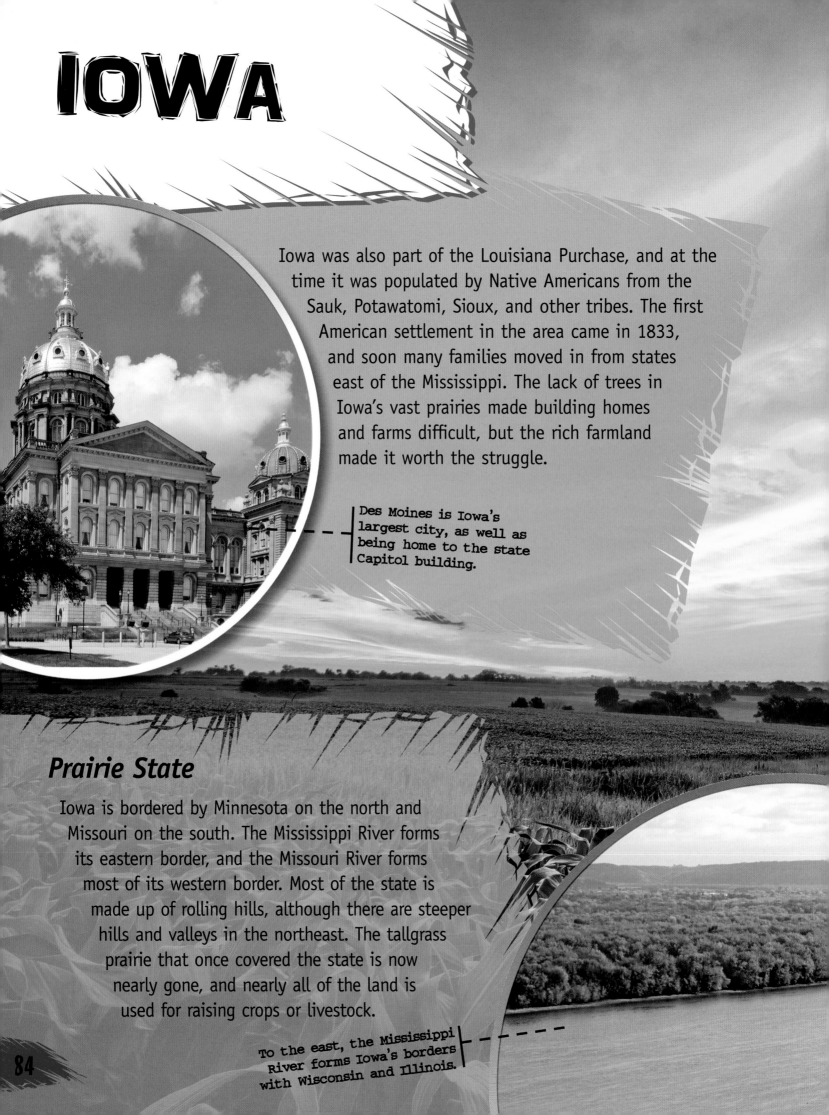

Iowa was also part of the Louisiana Purchase, and at the time it was populated by Native Americans from the Sauk, Potawatomi, Sioux, and other tribes. The first American settlement in the area came in 1833, and soon many families moved in from states east of the Mississippi. The lack of trees in Iowa's vast prairies made building homes and farms difficult, but the rich farmland made it worth the struggle.

Des Moines is Iowa's largest city, as well as being home to the state Capitol building.

Prairie State

Iowa is bordered by Minnesota on the north and Missouri on the south. The Mississippi River forms its eastern border, and the Missouri River forms most of its western border. Most of the state is made up of rolling hills, although there are steeper hills and valleys in the northeast. The tallgrass prairie that once covered the state is now nearly gone, and nearly all of the land is used for raising crops or livestock.

To the east, the Mississippi River forms Iowa's borders with Wisconsin and Illinois.

A Farming Powerhouse

Iowa's economy was built on farming, thanks to its rich soil. It produces more corn than any other state, and is second in soybean production. It is also a leader in hog and egg production, and has dozens of plants producing ethanol for fuel. However, manufacturing is also important, and many financial and insurance firms operate in Iowa.

IOWA FACT FILE

Admitted to Union: 1846 (the 29th state)
Capital: Des Moines
Rank in size: 26th
Rank in population: 30th
Nickname: Hawkeye State

Wind energy is a growing industry in Iowa, with turbines in many parts of the state.

Iowa's farms produce about 24 billion bushels of corn each year.

MISSOURI

Missouri was settled by the French, and the city of St. Louis, founded in 1764 at the **confluence** of the Mississippi and Missouri Rivers, soon became an important trading post for furs and other goods. In 1821, the Missouri Compromise allowed the state to enter the Union as a slave state, while Maine entered as a free state to keep the numbers balanced. Missouri did not join the Confederacy, but many Missourians supported it.

The Gateway Arch in St. Louis is a monument to the country's westward expansion.

Mark Twain based *The Adventures of Tom Sawyer* on his experiences growing up in Hannibal, Missouri

MISSOURI FACT FILE

Admitted to Union: 1821 (the 24th state)
Capital: Jefferson City
Rank in size: 21st
Rank in population: 18th
Nickname: Show-Me State

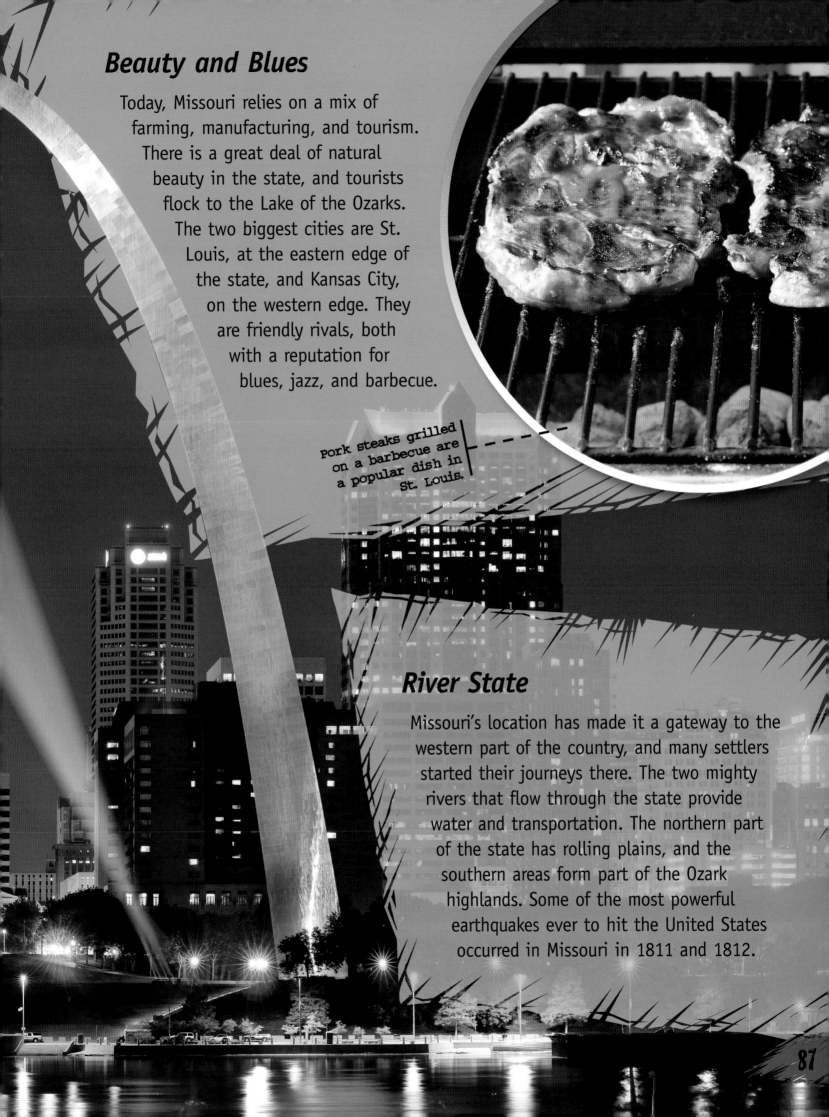

Beauty and Blues

Today, Missouri relies on a mix of farming, manufacturing, and tourism. There is a great deal of natural beauty in the state, and tourists flock to the Lake of the Ozarks. The two biggest cities are St. Louis, at the eastern edge of the state, and Kansas City, on the western edge. They are friendly rivals, both with a reputation for blues, jazz, and barbecue.

Pork steaks grilled on a barbecue are a popular dish in St. Louis.

River State

Missouri's location has made it a gateway to the western part of the country, and many settlers started their journeys there. The two mighty rivers that flow through the state provide water and transportation. The northern part of the state has rolling plains, and the southern areas form part of the Ozark highlands. Some of the most powerful earthquakes ever to hit the United States occurred in Missouri in 1811 and 1812.

KANSAS

Kansas was explored at various times by Spanish, French, and American explorers. Immigrants from the eastern part of the United States crossed through the state on their way west. When the region was opened up to settlement in 1854, many people wanted it to be a free territory, but others wanted it to be a slave territory. The issue of slavery led to bloody conflicts, and Kansas was only admitted as a free state in 1861, after many southern states had seceded.

Kansas leads the country in the production of wheat.

Agriculture and Airplanes

Kansas makes up part of the Great Plains, a region sometimes referred to as "America's Breadbasket." The farms in the eastern part of the state produce huge amounts of wheat, corn, and soybeans. The city of Wichita is known for manufacturing airplanes both large and small. The state is also gaining a reputation for renewable energy.

The aviation pioneer Amelia Earhart, who attempted to fly solo around the world, was from Kansas.

Plains and Trails

Kansas is bordered by Iowa to the north, Missouri to the east, Oklahoma to the south, and Colorado to the west. Large areas of the state are made up of flat or gently rolling plains, although the land rises in the west, near the border with Colorado. The National Park Service protects many historic sites, including trails used by settlers, the Pony Express, and the Lewis and Clark expedition.

These large chalk formations in northwest Kansas contain many fossils of prehistoric creatures.

KANSAS FACT FILE

Admitted to Union: 1861 (the 34th state)
Capital: Topeka
Rank in size: 15th
Rank in population: 33rd
Nickname: Sunflower State

89

NEBRASKA

Spanish and French traders came to the area that is now Nebraska to trade with the Native Americans who lived there. In the 1860s, the U.S. government opened up the territory to settlers and offered free land to those who wanted to set up farms. Thousands of people poured in. In the same decade, part of the Transcontinental Railroad was built across the territory, bringing yet more people to the new state.

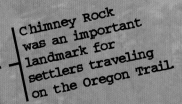

Chimney Rock was an important landmark for settlers traveling on the Oregon Trail

NEBRASKA FACT FILE

Admitted to Union: 1867 (the 37th state)
Capital: Lincoln
Rank in size: 16th
Rank in population: 38th
Nickname: Cornhusker State

Rivers and Dunes

The Platte River flows from west to east through the central part of the state, until it joins the Missouri River on the state's eastern border. The land in Nebraska is mainly flat or gently rolling, rising in the western part of the state. The region's rich soils are used for growing crops and grazing cattle, but in the northwest there is an area of plant-covered sand dunes called the Sandhills.

Because of the lack of trees, many settlers built their homes from blocks of sod.

In Nebraska, cows outnumber people by almost four to one.

Crops and Culture

Corn has always been an important crop in Nebraska—giving it the nickname of "The Cornhusker State"—but soybeans, wheat, and other crops are also grown. Nebraska is also a major producer of cattle and hogs. The state's factories have drawn immigrants from Mexico and Southeast Asia, giving the state a more diverse culture.

SOUTH DAKOTA

Before Europeans arrived, the land that is now South Dakota was dominated by the Sioux. Settlers started arriving in force in the 1850s, and when gold was discovered in the 1870s, even more came. Conflict with the Sioux led to several bloody battles, and in the end most of the Sioux were forced onto **reservations**. South Dakota suffered from drought in the 1930s, causing many people to leave the state.

Mount Rushmore shows the faces of four famous presidents. It is in the southwestern part of the state.

Split in Two

The Missouri River flows roughly north to south through the middle of South Dakota, dividing the state in half. The eastern part of the state is fairly flat, with low hills and lakes carved out by glaciers. In the west, the landscape is more rugged, with steep, flat-topped hills called buttes. The Black Hills, in the southwest, are a range of low mountains. They are rich in valuable minerals, such as copper, silver, and gold.

Badlands National Park protects the area's unusual rock formations and prairie habitats.

SOUTH DAKOTA FACT FILE

Admitted to Union: 1889 (the 40th state)
Capital: Pierre
Rank in size: 17th
Rank in population: 46th
Nickname: Mount Rushmore State

People and Places

Cattle and sheep ranching take up much of the land in South Dakota, and corn, wheat, and oats are also grown. Tourists come to see Mount Rushmore and the Wild West town of Deadwood. South Dakota has a large Sioux population, who have fought a long legal battle with the U.S. government over the ownership of the Black Hills.

The grasslands of South Dakota are home to many bison.

NORTH DAKOTA

North and South Dakota were both part of the Dakota Territory, which was occupied by Native American tribes such as the Sioux. Many homesteaders started to arrive in the 1860s and 1870s. The two areas became states on the same day: November 2, 1889. President Benjamin Harrison (1833–1901) deliberately shuffled the papers before signing, so that no one would know which state was officially approved first.

A monument in Rugby, North Dakota, marks the geographical center of North America.

Plains and Badlands

The landscape in North Dakota is similar to its southern neighbor, with hilly plains in the west and flatter river valleys in the east. In the western part of the state there are areas of **badlands**, some of which are protected as part of Theodore Roosevelt National Park. The state shares a long border with the Canadian provinces of Saskatchewan and Manitoba.

Theodore Roosevelt visited North Dakota's badlands in the 1880s, and the park that now protects them is named after him.

Wide Open Spaces

North Dakota is big in area, but fewer than one million people live there. The majority of the land is used for farming, and cereal crops such as barley, wheat, oats, and corn thrive there. North Dakota is the country's biggest producer of canola and sunflowers. The state also has significant deposits of natural gas, oil, and coal.

Sitting Bull was one of the chiefs who led the Sioux tribes in their defense of the Dakota Territory.

NORTH DAKOTA FACT FILE

Admitted to Union: 1889 (the 39th state)
Capital: Bismarck
Rank in size: 19th
Rank in population: 48th
Nickname: Peace Garden State

Fields of sunflowers are a common sight in many parts of North Dakota.

THE MOUNTAIN STATES

The majestic Rocky Mountains stretch for more than 3,000 miles, from Canada down to New Mexico. With many peaks reaching more than 13,000 feet, they form a barrier between the Pacific Coast and the flat prairies of the Great Plains. Several states have been carved out of this landscape, including Montana, Wyoming, Idaho, Colorado, Utah, and Nevada. The rugged terrain has given these states a unique character.

Cowboys are part of the history of the region, and they still exist today.

Exploring the Mountains

Although Native Americans had lived there for thousands of years, the Rockies were one of the last regions to be explored by Europeans. In the 19th century, explorers such as Meriwether Lewis (1774–1809) and William Clark (1770–1838), John C. Frémont (1813–1890), and Jedediah Smith (1799–1831) explored and mapped the region. Many settlers crossed the region to reach the Oregon Territory, and some stayed. In 1869, the transcontinental railroad provided an easier way to travel west.

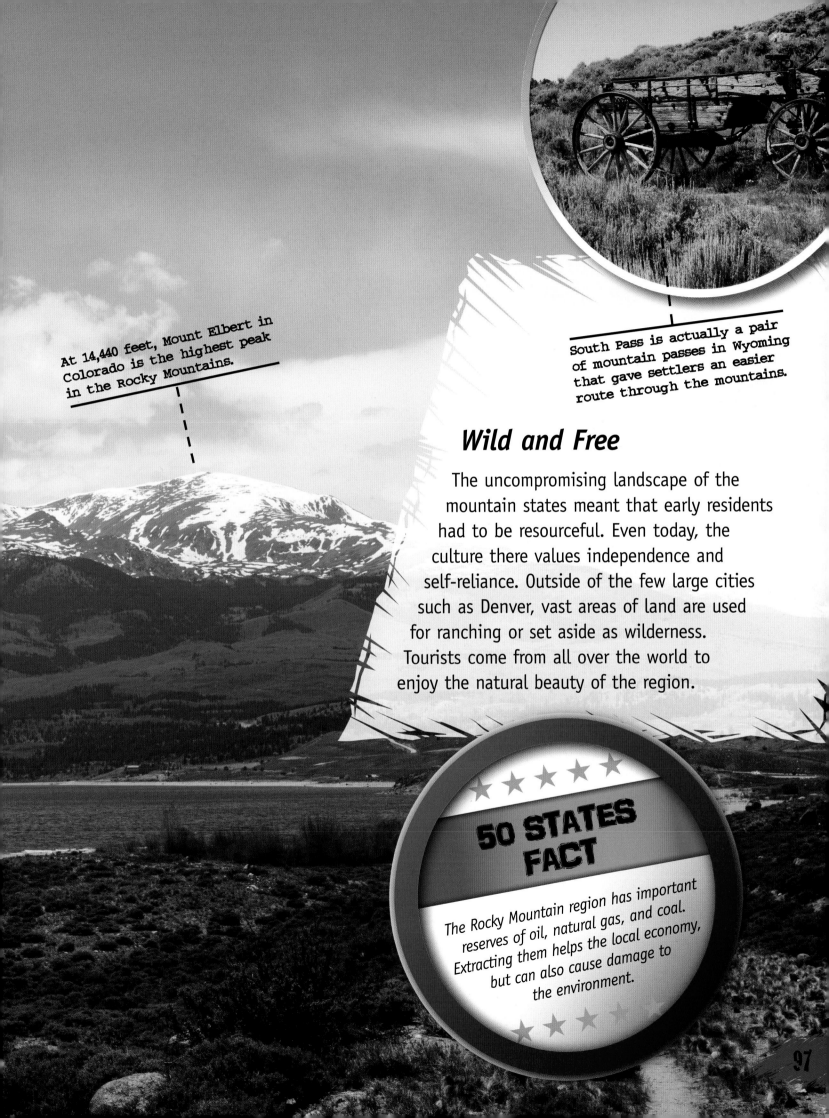

At 14,440 feet, Mount Elbert in Colorado is the highest peak in the Rocky Mountains.

South Pass is actually a pair of mountain passes in Wyoming that gave settlers an easier route through the mountains.

Wild and Free

The uncompromising landscape of the mountain states meant that early residents had to be resourceful. Even today, the culture there values independence and self-reliance. Outside of the few large cities such as Denver, vast areas of land are used for ranching or set aside as wilderness. Tourists come from all over the world to enjoy the natural beauty of the region.

★★★★★ 50 STATES FACT

The Rocky Mountain region has important reserves of oil, natural gas, and coal. Extracting them helps the local economy, but can also cause damage to the environment.

MONTANA

The land that is now Montana was home to Native American tribes such as the Crow, Cheyenne, and Blackfeet. Then settlers started to move into the area, first to trade furs, and later to mine for gold, silver, and other minerals. There were many conflicts over control of the land. The Battle of the Little Bighorn (1876), one of the most famous battles between the U.S. Army and Native Americans, was fought in Montana.

Open pit mines in Montana have dug deep into the ground

Mountain State

Montana gets its name from the Spanish word for "mountain," and it is not hard to see why. The western half of the state is crisscrossed by dozens of mountain ranges, with rich river valleys separating some of them. There are prairies and plains in the eastern part of the state. Glacier National Park, a stunning area of mountains, glaciers, and lakes, is in the northwest.

MONTANA FACT FILE

Admitted to Union: 1889 (the 41st state)
Capital: Helena
Rank in size: 4th
Rank in population: 44th
Nickname: Treasure State

Wild and Beautiful

Montana's economy is based on crops, livestock, mining, timber, and tourism. In addition to cattle, Montana's ranches raise more unusual animals such as ostriches and emus. The state's vast open lands provide a habitat for grizzly bears, bison, mountain goats, bald eagles, and more. Tourists come to try out western skills such as horseriding and driving cattle.

There are currently about 800 grizzly bears in Montana.

Glacier National Park protects more than 1 million acres of wilderness.

WYOMING

Native American tribes such as the Shoshone, Arapahoe, and Cheyenne lived in the area that is now Wyoming. The first American to explore the area was probably John Colter (1774–1813), who had been a member of the Lewis and Clark expedition. They did not visit Wyoming, but he described the region a few years later, in 1807. However, many people did not believe his stories of the state's unique natural wonders.

Rodeo is the official state sport in Wyoming, and it attracts thousands of spectators.

Equality and Industry

Wyoming has fewer people than any other state, but it has a reputation for equality. In 1869, it became the first part of the United States to give women the right to vote. In 1925, it elected the first woman **governor**. Today, the state's biggest industries are tourism, agriculture, and mining. Wyoming produces coal, oil, natural gas, and uranium.

Wyoming granted women the right to vote and serve on juries when it was still a territory.

The Teton Mountains are one of the most beautiful ranges in Wyoming.

WYOMING FACT FILE

Admitted to Union: 1890 (the 44th state)
Capital: Cheyenne
Rank in size: 10th
Rank in population: 50th
Nickname: Equality State

Old Faithful is the most famous geyser at Yellowstone, erupting once every one or two hours.

Mountains and Geysers

Wyoming is a high plateau broken up by several mountain ranges, such as the Grand Tetons. Rivers such as the Snake and the Yellowstone flow across the state. Wyoming's crowning jewel is Yellowstone National Park. This area sits on top of a "hotspot," where molten rock from deep within the planet comes closer to the surface than normal. This underground heat has produced geysers and hot springs, making Yellowstone like no other place in the country.

IDAHO

Archeologists have found evidence of human hunters living in the Idaho region more than 10,000 years ago. By the time that Europeans arrived, it was home to the Nez Perce and the Shoshone. Many of the early explorers were French-Canadian fur trappers, who gave French names to many settlements and landforms. The territory was claimed by both the United States and the British until 1846.

Sacagawea, who helped to guide the Lewis and Clark expedition, was a Shoshone from the region that is now Idaho.

IDAHO FACT FILE

Admitted to Union: 1890 (the 43rd state)
Capital: Boise
Rank in size: 14th
Rank in population: 39th
Nickname: Gem State

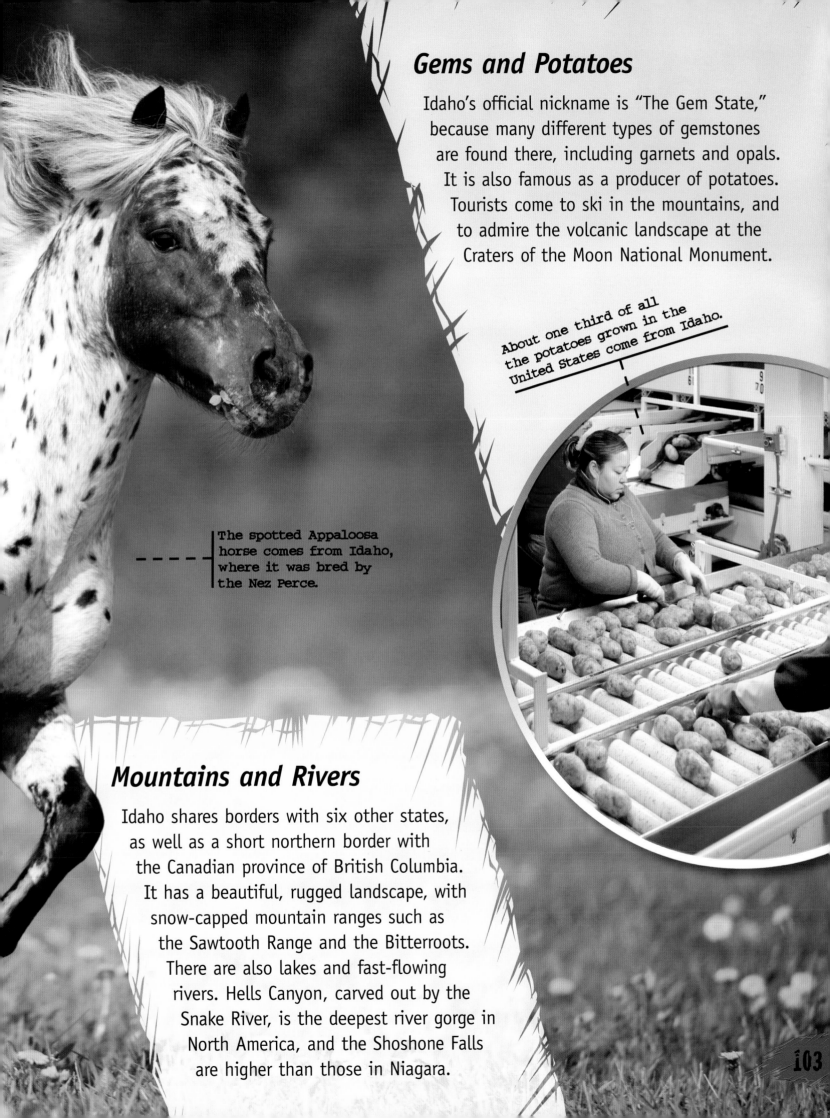

Gems and Potatoes

Idaho's official nickname is "The Gem State," because many different types of gemstones are found there, including garnets and opals. It is also famous as a producer of potatoes. Tourists come to ski in the mountains, and to admire the volcanic landscape at the Craters of the Moon National Monument.

About one third of all the potatoes grown in the United States come from Idaho.

The spotted Appaloosa horse comes from Idaho, where it was bred by the Nez Perce.

Mountains and Rivers

Idaho shares borders with six other states, as well as a short northern border with the Canadian province of British Columbia. It has a beautiful, rugged landscape, with snow-capped mountain ranges such as the Sawtooth Range and the Bitterroots. There are also lakes and fast-flowing rivers. Hells Canyon, carved out by the Snake River, is the deepest river gorge in North America, and the Shoshone Falls are higher than those in Niagara.

COLORADO

Many tribes of Native Americans have lived in Colorado for thousands of years. The United States claimed part of the region as part of the Louisiana Purchase, but Spain had possession of the rest. Fur trappers and settlers set up towns and trading posts, where they traded items such as buffalo hides with the Native Americans. In 1848, the whole region became part of the United States.

Native Americans left behind cliff dwellings at Mesa Verde.

COLORADO FACT FILE

Admitted to Union: 1876 (the 38th state)
Capital: Denver
Rank in size: 8th
Rank in population: 22nd
Nickname: Centennial State

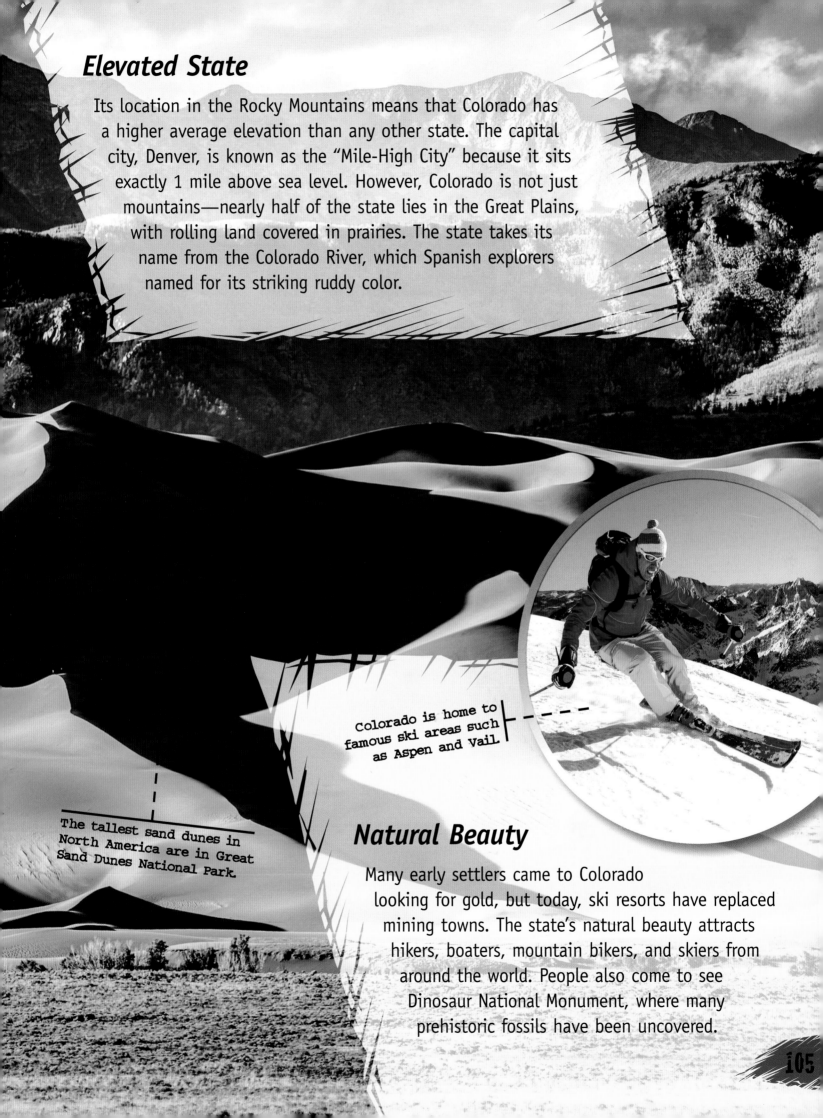

Elevated State

Its location in the Rocky Mountains means that Colorado has a higher average elevation than any other state. The capital city, Denver, is known as the "Mile-High City" because it sits exactly 1 mile above sea level. However, Colorado is not just mountains—nearly half of the state lies in the Great Plains, with rolling land covered in prairies. The state takes its name from the Colorado River, which Spanish explorers named for its striking ruddy color.

Colorado is home to famous ski areas such as Aspen and Vail.

The tallest sand dunes in North America are in Great Sand Dunes National Park.

Natural Beauty

Many early settlers came to Colorado looking for gold, but today, ski resorts have replaced mining towns. The state's natural beauty attracts hikers, boaters, mountain bikers, and skiers from around the world. People also come to see Dinosaur National Monument, where many prehistoric fossils have been uncovered.

UTAH

Although Native Americans and Spanish explorers both lived in Utah before U.S. settlers arrived, the state's history is most linked with one particular group: the Church of Jesus Christ of Latter-Day Saints, better known as the Mormons. They began moving to Utah in the 1840s, looking for a place where they could practice their religion in peace. More settlers arrived from the eastern states, and Utah became a state in 1896.

The Great Salt Lake is the largest saltwater lake in the Northern Hemisphere.

From Desert to Mountain

Utah's landscape is incredibly varied. There are mountains, including the Wasatch Range, in the north. The western part of the state is part of the Great Basin, made up of arid desert and smaller mountain ranges. The southern and southeastern areas are part of the Colorado Plateau, where sandstone has been eroded over millions of years into fantastic shapes.

Arches National Park has more than 2,000 natural stone arches.

Old and New

Utah has changed a lot, but Mormons still make up more than 60 percent of the population, giving the state a unique culture. A growing Hispanic population is making the state more diverse. Mining and cattle ranching are important industries, and so is tourism. Utah has several world-class ski areas, as well as stunning national parks including Arches, Bryce Canyon, and Zion.

Located in Salt Lake City, the Salt Lake Temple is the center of the Mormon religion.

NEVADA

The glitzy casinos of the Las Vegas Strip try to outdo each other to attract visitors.

Spanish explorers gave this region the name "Nevada," which means "snowy," because of the snow that covered its mountains in the winter. The territory became part of the United States in 1848, but settlers were slow to arrive, probably due to the harsh, arid climate. All that changed when silver was discovered in 1859. Miners swarmed in from all over, hoping to strike it rich.

The remains of abandoned mines can still be seen in Nevada today.

Dry and Rugged

More than 30 rugged mountain ranges run north to south across Nevada's landscape, with flat valleys between them. The land is lower in the southern part of the state, which is located within the Mojave Desert. There are several beautiful lakes, such as Lake Tahoe, but Nevada is the driest state in the United States. Plants and animals in Nevada must have adaptations to cope with extreme temperatures and lack of water.

Beautiful Lake Tahoe, on the border with California, is surrounded by mountains and pine forests.

Hilton Grand Vacations

NEVADA FACT FILE

★ ★ ★ ★ ★

Admitted to Union: 1864 (the 36th state)
Capital: Carson City
Rank in size: 7th
Rank in population: 35th
Nickname: Silver State

★ ★ ★ ★

Mining and Gambling

Nevada was built on mining, but today the state is famous for its tourism. The state government legalized gambling in 1931, hoping that it would pull Nevada out of the Great Depression. Since then, tourism has become a huge part of the economy. People go to Las Vegas and Reno for its casinos, theaters, and sporting events.

Hoover Dam, which lies on the Colorado River on the Arizona–Nevada border, provides electricity for three states.

109

THE SOUTHWEST

The Southwest is an area with borders that are hard to define. Some people would include Colorado, Utah, and Nevada in this region, or exclude Texas and Oklahoma. The states in this area share a similar landscape and climate, as well as a cultural history. Most regions were originally settled by the Spanish, who lived side by side with the local Native Americans.

The sandstone rock formations at Monument Valley are all that remain after erosion wore away the surrounding rock.

Natural Beauty

The Southwest is home to some of the country's most stunning landscapes. From the awe-inspiring Grand Canyon, surrounded by dense pine forests, to the cactus-strewn deserts of the southern regions, this area really is like nowhere else on Earth. Part of the region lies on the Colorado Plateau, an area of high land crisscrossed with canyons and rivers. To the east, the landscape shifts to plains and prairies.

The saguaro cactuses found in southwest Arizona can grow to more than 70 feet tall

The Grand Canyon cuts through layers of colored rock. It is over 1 mile deep in places.

Rich Culture

Mining, ranching, and farming were traditionally the main industries in the Southwest. More recently, the region's warm climate and natural attractions have led to the rise of tourism. Artists such as Georgia O'Keeffe (1887–1986) have found inspiration in the Southwest. The mix of cultures such as Native American, Hispanic, and European has an influence on the region's arts, food, and music.

Chaco Canyon contains the remains of large building complexes that were built by Native American people about 1,000 years ago.

50 STATES FACT

The Southwest has a huge variety of plants and animals. The Gila monster is the only venomous species of lizard found in the United States.

OKLAHOMA

The land that is now Oklahoma was claimed by Spain in the 16th century and then joined the United States as part of the Louisiana Purchase. In 1828, the government set the land aside for Native Americans who were being forced from their homes farther east. The land was opened up to European settlers in 1889. During the 1930s, a drought called the "Dust Bowl" forced farmers to move away.

On September 16, 1893, more than 100,000 settlers raced to claim land in Oklahoma.

Plains and Wind

The northeastern part of the state, where it borders Arkansas and Missouri, is made up of highlands that are part of the Ozark Plateau. The Ouachita Mountains are in the southeast. To the west of these areas are sandstone hills, where oil has been found. The western part of the state is mainly **fertile** plains and low hills, with some forests. Oklahoma's location and climate cause frequent tornadoes.

Animals such as antelope, coyotes, and elk are found in Oklahoma's landscape.

Cowboy State

In the 19th century, Oklahoma became a homeland for many different Native American tribes, and it still has a high percentage of Native Americans living there. The state was also a center for cattle ranching, and cowboy culture is alive and well today. In the 20th century, Oklahoma's economy depended on oil and gas, as well as agriculture.

Oklahoma is the only state to have a working oil rig on the grounds of its Capitol building.

Much of Oklahoma lies in an area called "Tornado Alley" because of the tornadoes that tear through it.

★★★★★
OKLAHOMA FACT FILE

Admitted to Union: 1907 (the 46th state)
Capital: Oklahoma City
Rank in size: 20th
Rank in population: 28th
Nickname: Sooner State

★★★★

TEXAS

Texas is one of the few states that were once independent countries. After being explored by the Spanish in the 16th century and the French in the 17th century, the land was claimed by Mexico in the 18th century. Texas won its independence from Mexico in 1836, and formed a republic, before joining the United States in 1845. During the Civil War it seceded to join the Confederacy. The flags of six nations have flown over Texas.

The Alamo was the site of a famous battle in 1836. The Texans lost the battle, but they won their independence from Mexico later that year.

Big and Varied

Texas is bigger than any other state except for Alaska, and its size means that its geography is incredibly diverse. In the southeast there are fertile coastal plains, perfect for farming and cattle ranching. Near the Gulf of Mexico, the land is more marshy. To the west and northwest there are high plains and mountains. The Rio Grande flows along the southwest, forming a long border with Mexico.

Chili is an example of the "Tex Mex" cuisine that the state is famous for.

At the beginning of the 20th century, large oil deposits were discovered in Texas, changing the state's economy forever.

Oil and Cattle

Texas leads the nation in oil and natural gas production, and it also leads the country in wind energy. The state's farms and ranches produce cotton, vegetables, fruit, cattle, sheep, and goats. Texas has a diverse culture with a large Mexican-American population. Texans are proud of their state, and sometimes claim that everything is bigger—and better—in Texas.

TEXAS FACT FILE

Admitted to Union: 1845 (the 28th state)
Capital: Austin
Rank in size: 2nd
Rank in population: 2nd
Nickname: Lone Star State

NEW MEXICO

Spanish explorers came to the land that is now New Mexico in 1540, looking for legendary cities of gold. They did not find gold, but later explorers set up cities such as Santa Fe, which was founded in 1610. The land remained under Spanish control until 1821, when it became part of Mexico. The United States won the territory from Mexico in 1848.

Many buildings in Santa Fe and other parts of New Mexico are made from a type of mud brick called adobe.

NEW MEXICO FACT FILE

Admitted to Union: 1912 (the 47th state)
Capital: Santa Fe
Rank in size: 5th
Rank in population: 36th
Nickname: Land of Enchantment

The beautiful dunes of White Sands National Monument get their color from gypsum crystals.

Deserts and Caverns

New Mexico is a mix of flat land, rugged mountains, pine forests, and desert. The eastern part of the state is part of the Great Plains, and the Rocky Mountains cover the north-central area. The Rio Grande flows from north to south, passing through the city of Albuquerque. The fantastic caves of Carlsbad Caverns lie hidden beneath the desert in the southeast.

Carlsbad Caverns feature many columns, stalactites, stalagmites, and other limestone formations.

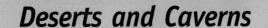

Mix of Cultures

New Mexico's culture has been shaped by the different groups that have lived there over the centuries: Spanish, Mexican, and European settlers, as well as Native Americans including the Navajo and Pueblo. Tourists come to experience the state's natural wonders and unique culture. New Mexico's food is a fusion of Spanish, Mexican, Native American, and cowboy influences, and is famous for its blue corn and red and green chile sauces.

ARIZONA

Native Americans from the Hopi, Hohokam, Pueblo, and other cultures lived in Arizona long before the Spanish arrived in the 16th century. The explorers looked for gold and tried to convert the local people to Christianity. Like its neighbor, New Mexico, Arizona became part of Mexico in 1821, was passed to the United States in 1848, and finally became a state in 1912.

London Bridge spanned the River Thames, in England, before being dismantled and reassembled in Lake Havasu City, Arizona.

Canyon State

The northern part of Arizona is part of the Colorado Plateau, with beautiful rock formations and pine forests. The spectacular Grand Canyon, carved out by the Colorado River, is part of this area. To the south, the land flattens out into a hot desert region marked by large cactuses. Arizona's largest cities, such as Phoenix and Tucson, are in this part of the state.

The Barringer Crater formed when a giant meteorite crashed into Earth millions of years ago in an area that is now near Winslow, Arizona.

Arizona's capital, Phoenix, is one of the fastest-growing cities in the country.

Arizona's Economy

In the past, Arizona's economy depended on mining, lumber, cattle ranching, and growing crops such as cotton and alfalfa. That has changed in recent decades, and now the state has a thriving high-tech industry. It also depends heavily on tourism. People come from around the world to see the Grand Canyon, as well as other national parks such as Petrified Forest and Saguaro.

Petrified Forest National Park features the remains of trees that lived over 200 million years ago.

ARIZONA FACT FILE

Admitted to Union: 1912 (the 48th state)
Capital: Phoenix
Rank in size: 6th
Rank in population: 16th
Nickname: Grand Canyon State

THE PACIFIC COAST

Many people drive along California's Pacific Coast Highway for the stunning views.

The Pacific Coast is about 3,000 miles west of the Atlantic Coast, where the first colonies were founded. The first European explorers arrived by ship. Although the explorers Lewis and Clark traveled over land to reach the Pacific in 1805, it was several decades before settlers started to arrive in large numbers. But once they did, they displaced the local populations of Native Americans.

Giant sequoia trees grow near the California coast.

50 STATES FACT

Hawaii is located in the Pacific Ocean, but its Polynesian heritage gives it a distinct culture. Likewise, Alaska's isolation and rugged natural environment have shaped the state's character.

Coastal Geography

The Pacific Coast stretches about 1,300 miles from Washington down to southern California. Farther north, Alaska has more than 5,000 miles of coastline. A range of coastal mountains runs along the edge of California, Oregon, and Washington. The coastal states have **temperate rain forests** in the north and deserts in the south. Hawaii and Alaska have their own unique geographies.

The islands of Hawaii have many sandy beaches.

West Coast Culture

Over the years, the states of the Pacific Coast—and California in particular—have developed their own unique culture. West Coast residents have a reputation for being informal and laid-back, often with progressive views. The natural wonders of the area have led many people to work hard to protect the beautiful environment, and organizations such as the Sierra Club began there.

CALIFORNIA

Spanish explorers were the first Europeans to colonize California, where they tried to convert the Native Americans to Christianity. Settlers from the United States started to arrive in 1841, drawn by the area's natural riches. The United States soon declared war on Mexico, and when they eventually won, they got California as part of the settlement. About a year later, the discovery of gold sparked a gold rush that changed the state's history.

Prospectors hoped to strike it rich in California's gold rush.

Mountains and Valleys

The towering mountain range known as the Sierra Nevada runs from north to south along California's eastern edge. The mountains of the Coast Ranges run along the Pacific Coast. The fertile Central Valley, with some of the richest farmland in the country, lies between the two ranges. The Mojave Desert is in the southeast, and it includes Death Valley, the lowest point in the United States.

There are thousands of wineries in California, which account for 90% of the wine produced in the United States.

Nature and Culture

California really does have it all: thriving cities such as San Francisco and Los Angeles, rugged natural wonders, beautiful beaches, and a vibrant culture enhanced by waves of immigration over the years. The state is known for producing wine as well as fruits and vegetables, and it is the home of Hollywood, which produces movies and television shows that are watched around the world.

San Francisco is a port city with a rich history and a diverse culture.

CALIFORNIA FACT FILE

Admitted to Union: 1850 (the 31st state)
Capital: Sacramento
Rank in size: 3rd
Rank in population: 1st
Nickname: Golden State

OREGON

Native American tribes such as the Chinook and Klamath lived in the region that is now Oregon. Francis Drake (1540–1596) claimed the area for England in 1579, but the area stayed largely unexplored until Lewis and Clark traveled through it, reaching the Pacific Coast in 1805. Starting in 1830, settlers from the eastern states traveled along the Oregon Trail to reach its rich lands. It became a U.S. territory in 1846, and a state in 1859.

Oregon was a popular destination for settlers moving west, who often traveled in covered wagons.

OREGON FACT FILE

Admitted to Union: 1859 (the 33rd state)
Capital: Salem
Rank in size: 9th
Rank in population: 27th
Nickname: Beaver State

Forest State

Crater Lake formed in the remains of an ancient volcano. It is the deepest lake in the United States.

The beautiful Cascade Mountains run north to south through the state, and they include many lakes. The lower Coast Range lies along the coast, and between the two is the fertile Willamette Valley. Many of the state's mountains are covered with forests of spruce, fir, and hemlock trees. The mighty Columbia River forms part of the boundary between Oregon and Washington. Part of the state is made up of a temperate rain forest.

Logging and Technology

For many years, Oregon's vast forests were the basis of its economy, producing lumber, paper, plywood, and other products. Now, industries such as tourism, manufacturing, and technology are starting to take over. Oregon has a reputation for protecting the environment and for liberal attitudes. Portland, the largest city, is a dynamic place known for its cafes and food trucks.

The beaver is the state animal of Oregon, as well as being the source of its nickname.

WASHINGTON

Native Americans such as the Chinook and Salish tribes lived in Washington, where they farmed, hunted, and fished. When European explorers arrived, they set up a thriving trade in sea otter skins. Both American and British citizens were allowed to settle and trade there until 1846, when it became part of the United States. Washington became a state in 1889, named for President George Washington.

Mountains and Rain Forests

Puget Sound, an inlet of the Pacific Ocean, digs into the northwestern corner of the state, creating the mountainous Olympic Peninsula. There are lowlands surrounding the sound, and to the east of these are the Cascade Mountains, which include several volcanoes. In the southeast part of the state there are rolling hills with fertile soil. There are temperate rain forests in the western part of the state, but east of the Cascades the climate is drier.

Sol Duc Falls trail is found in the rain forest in the Olympic National Park, Washington.

Mount Rainier, the tallest mountain in Washington, is an active volcano.

WASHINGTON FACT FILE

Admitted to Union: 1889 (the 42nd state)
Capital: Olympia
Rank in size: 18th
Rank in population: 13th
Nickname: Evergreen State

Washington's Economy

For a long time, Washington's economy depended on four "F"s: fur, farming, forests, and fishing. Now the state is embracing new technologies. Microsoft has its headquarters in Washington, and for many years so did the aircraft manufacturer Boeing. Tourists come to enjoy whale watching in Puget Sound, as well as hiking, skiing, and mountain biking.

Seattle, Washington's largest city, has trendy cafes and a thriving music scene.

ALASKA

Alaska is the biggest state in the country, as well as the farthest north. Native groups such as the Aleuts and Tlingit lived there undisturbed until the 18th century, when Russian explorers and fur traders arrived. They competed with British and American traders until 1867, when Russia sold the territory to the United States. A gold rush in the late 19th century brought many settlers to the area.

Alaska contains some of the highest peaks in the United States.

Arctic Landscape

Alaska is one of only two states that do not border any others. Instead, it shares a long land border with Canada. The Aleutian Islands stretch out toward Russia across the Bering Sea. Alaska has many mountain ranges, as well as glaciers, dense forests, and river valleys. The northern part of the state lies inside the Arctic Circle, where trees cannot grow and the soil is almost permanently frozen.

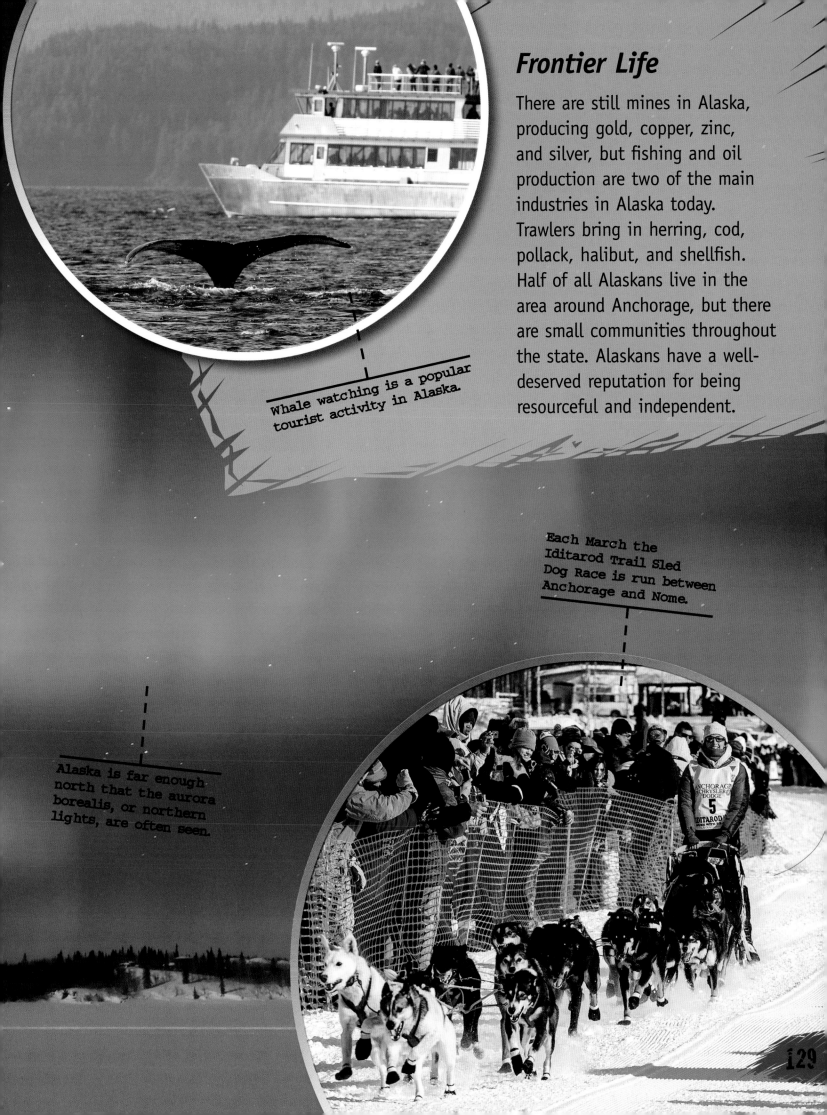

Frontier Life

There are still mines in Alaska, producing gold, copper, zinc, and silver, but fishing and oil production are two of the main industries in Alaska today. Trawlers bring in herring, cod, pollack, halibut, and shellfish. Half of all Alaskans live in the area around Anchorage, but there are small communities throughout the state. Alaskans have a well-deserved reputation for being resourceful and independent.

Whale watching is a popular tourist activity in Alaska.

Each March the Iditarod Trail Sled Dog Race is run between Anchorage and Nome.

Alaska is far enough north that the aurora borealis, or northern lights, are often seen.

129

HaWaii

Diamond Head, which looms over Honolulu, is the remains of an ancient volcano.

The first Hawaiians arrived by canoe across the Pacific Ocean about 1,500 years ago. In 1778, Captain James Cook (1728–1779) of Great Britain became the first European to visit Hawaii. After that, missionaries and whalers from Britain and the United States began to arrive. They gained more and more power, until they overthrew the government of Queen Liliuokalani (1838–1917) in 1893. Hawaii became the 50th state in 1959.

Volcano State

Hawaii is a long archipelago in the Pacific Ocean, made up of eight main islands and more than 100 smaller ones. The islands were formed by volcanoes erupting from the sea floor. A few volcanoes, such as Mauna Loa and Kilauea, are still active. In some places the pounding waves have pulverized the lava, creating unusual black sand beaches. Hawaii's isolated location means that it has species of plants and animals found nowhere else on Earth.

Lava flows slowly over the land, turning black as it cools and forms rock.

East and West

In the last 200 years, Hawaii's Polynesian population has mixed with immigrants from China, Japan, the Philippines, the United States, and elsewhere, creating a unique culture with a mix of East and West. Tourism is the biggest industry, as people arrive to enjoy the state's mild climate, natural beauty, and fantastic surfing beaches.

Pineapples are one of Hawaii's main crops.

HAWAII FACT FILE

Admitted to Union: 1959 (the 50th state)
Capital: Honolulu
Rank in size: 43rd
Rank in population: 40th
Nickname: Aloha State

WASHINGTON, DC

The United States needed a capital where the government could meet. During the fight for independence, the founders had met in Philadelphia, New York, and other cities. But they wanted a permanent capital that was not part of any state, so that it could represent all states equally. Virginia and Maryland each gave up a bit of land to form the District of Columbia. This area, where the city of Washington now stands, is a federal district, not a state.

The cherry trees that line the banks of the Tidal Basin were a gift from the mayor of Tokyo, Japan, in 1912.

Planning a City

Everything about the new city was carefully planned. Its location connected north and south, as well as forming a bridge from the east coast to the western frontier. Architects and surveyors planned out an elegant, well-organized city. Before long, work started on impressive buildings such as the White House, Capitol, and Supreme Court Building. The city is now a thriving city in its own right, as well as being the seat of government.

Cultural Gems

As the nation's capital, Washington, DC is full of historical treasures. These include working buildings, such as the Capitol where Congress meets, as well as monuments and memorials that celebrate the nation's history, such as the Vietnam Veterans Memorial and the Washington Monument. Washington also has many museums, theaters, and performing arts venues.

The United States Capitol has two main wings: one for the Senate and one for the House of Representatives.

The Smithsonian Institution is a group of museums overseen by the federal government.

WASHINGTON, DC FACT FILE

Founded: 1790
Area: 68 square miles
Population: 672,228
Designed by:
Pierre Charles L'Enfant

BECOMING A STATE

Congress would have to approve any new states joining the Union.

During some parts of the nation's history, states were added at an astonishing rate, filling up the land between the East and West Coasts. But since 1959, no new states have joined. The last two, Alaska and Hawaii, have shown that states do not necessarily need to be near the rest of the country. But how exactly does a state join the Union? And will there ever be a 51st state?

50 STATES FACT

Between 1816 and 1821, a new state was added each year. In 1889, four new states joined the Union in less than two weeks!

How to Join

The U.S. Constitution set up the rules for new states joining the Union and gave Congress the authority to admit new states. In most cases, a territory would hold a vote called a referendum to see whether most residents supported statehood. If the referendum passed, the territory's government would then write a state constitution. If Congress accepted the constitution, it would admit the territory as a state.

Many people campaign to make Washington, DC a state.

Who Is Next?

The District of Columbia is not a state, so it has no representatives or **senators** to give its residents a voice in government. Because of this, many residents of Washington, DC would like to see their home become a state. There are also many people in the territory of Puerto Rico who would like to apply for statehood.

The island of Puerto Rico may one day become a state.

STATE GOVERNMENTS

While the federal government headquartered in Washington, DC oversees the nation as a whole, each of the 50 states has its own government. The Constitution states that any powers that are not assigned to the federal government will fall under the control of the state governments. States can pass their own laws, but they must not go against federal laws.

Each state is run by a governor, such as Nikki Haley of South Carolina.

Like all states, Utah has its own supreme court, which meets in this building.

★★★★★
50 STATES FACT

Although they are called by different names, most states have a legislature with two houses. Nebraska is the only state with just one, which is usually called the Senate.

450

Three Branches

No two state governments are identical, but they all share certain similarities. The state governments all have the same three branches as the federal system: executive, legislative, and judicial. The executive branch is headed by the governor, whose role is similar to the president's. The legislative branch is made up of elected representatives, who make laws. The judicial branch has different levels of law courts.

People in each state vote to choose their state governors and representatives.

Who Does What?

The federal government has many powers, including printing money and making treaties with foreign governments. States make laws about issues such as crime, welfare, divorce and family matters, and business contracts. However, there are some powers that are shared by the federal and state governments. For example, both can collect taxes, establish courts, and build highways.

137

WORKING TOGETHER

The 50 states have some degree of independence, but they work together to keep the nation running, protect the environment, and ensure equal rights for all citizens. No matter what state a person is from, they have the same rights and privileges in any of the other 49.

The diverse populations of the 50 states give the country its unique identity.

National defense is organized by the federal government.

Congress

Each state's residents vote on elected officials to represent them in the federal government. Every state has two senators, who serve six-year terms in the U.S. Senate. The number of representatives to Congress depends on a state's population: the bigger the state, the more representatives it has. So, for example, Vermont has only one, but California, which has the largest population of any state, has 53. Representatives serve two-year terms.

Registering vehicles and issuing license plates are done by the state governments.

Crossing Boundaries

For most of its history, the United States has been full of people on the move. Although many families stayed in the same region for generations, others moved long distances to find land, jobs, or more freedom. Today, better communication and transportation mean that even more people are moving from one state to another. Large companies also set up offices, stores, or factories in many different states.

50 STATES FACT

In the 2010 census, 79 percent of the residents of Louisiana were born in the state. In contrast, only 24 percent of Nevada's residents were born there. The rest immigrated from elsewhere.

GLOSSARY

Amendment A change to a law or official document. The United States Constitution has 27 amendments.

Badlands Areas where water has eroded the land into deep gullies and unusual rock formations.

Barrier islands Long, sandy islands that run along shores and protect them from the ocean.

Civil rights movement A campaign during the 1950s and 1960s that tried to end discrimination against African Americans.

Civil War The war fought from 1861–1865 between the states of the North and the states of the South.

Colonies Areas that are controlled by a country that is usually far away from them.

Confederacy (Confederate States of America) The group of Southern states that seceded from the United States during the Civil War to form their own country.

Confluence The place where two rivers join to become one.

Congress The body in the United States government responsible for making laws.

Constitution A document that describes the system of laws by which a country is governed.

Continental Congress A group of men from the 13 colonies who served as the country's government during the Revolutionary War.

Delta A triangular piece of land formed when a river splits into smaller rivers before flowing into an ocean.

Dialects Forms of language that are spoken in particular areas.

Elevation A measure of how high above sea level a place is.

Federal government The government of the United States as a whole, as opposed to the governments of the individual states.

Fertile Able to produce many plants or crops.

Frontier A wild area where few people live, at the edge of a settled territory.

Glaciers Large bodies of ice that move slowly down a slope or valley.

Governor The person who is the leader of the government of a state.

Great Lakes The chain of five large lakes on the border of the United States and Canada.

Hurricanes Very large, powerful storms with strong winds that form over the ocean.

Ice age A time in the distant past when a large part of the world was covered with ice.

Immigrants People who come to a country to live there permanently.

Louisiana Purchase A large area of land west of the Mississippi River that the United States government bought from France in 1803.

Northwest Territory A former region of the United States that includes all or parts of Ohio, Indiana, Illinois, Michigan, Wisconsin, and Minnesota.

Oregon Trail A long route stretching from Missouri to Oregon.

Panhandle A part of a land area that is narrow and sticks out from a larger area.

Peninsula A piece of land that is attached to a larger land area but almost entirely surrounded by water.

Piedmont A region at the base of the Appalachian Mountains.

Pilgrims The people who traveled by boat from England to land in Massachusetts in 1620.

Plateau A large, flat area of high land.

Prairies Large, mostly flat lands with few trees that are covered in grasses.

Quakers A Christian group that is also known as the Religious Society of Friends.

Ratify To make a law or agreement official by signing or voting for it.

Representatives Members of the House of Representatives of the U.S. Congress or of a state government.

Republic A country that is governed by elected representatives instead of by a king or queen.

Reservations Areas of land that are set aside as places for Native Americans to live.

Revolutionary War The war fought by the 13 colonies against the British king and government from 1775–1783.

Secede To separate from a country and become independent.

Senators Elected representatives that are members of the U.S. Senate or of a state senate.

Settlers People who go to live in a new place.

Slavery The system in which a person is owned by another person and forced to work for them without pay.

Taxes Amounts of money that a government requires people or companies to pay.

Temperate rain forests Woodland areas in a temperate climate zone that receive heavy rainfall.

Territory One of the parts of the United States that is not a state.

Trappers People who trap animals in order to sell their fur.

Union A group of states that are ruled by one government or that agree to work together. "Union" can refer either to the United States as a whole, or to the Northern states that fought against the Confederacy in the Civil War.

INDEX